Table of Contents

A Quick Note

I write like I talk. And as you read this book from beginning to end, you may notice that I repeat and review some important lessons. Understand the reason is that I think the lesson is paramount to your success.

This book can be read straight through or as a reference on an as-needed basis, to identify more relevant training to your individual situation.

Special Thanks

There are a few people I want to thank for supporting me in my business venture.

The first person I want to thank is my wife, Laura. She has been with me through the thick and the thin, when times were tough and when times were good, and always has been a rock of support.

I also want to thank Mom and Dad, both unique in their ways as parents, but both helpful in being there for me and helping me out through my childhood and into my adult life.

I want all of the agencies that have supported me along the way. You know who you are and I appreciate you.

A special thanks to my original trainer, Andrew Fike. Andrew taught me most of how I present the differences between term versus whole life final expense coverage.

I also want to thank Tim Winders. Tim is a tour de force in the final expense business, much of my approach to pre-qualification was originated from his final expense presentation.

Lastly, I want to thank John Dugger in Kentucky. John is a fantastic agent who has had much success in this business with his low-key approach to selling.

John has tirelessly given much of his time to help new final expense agents sell more, and I as well as many agents owe him a debt of gratitude for his advice and counsel.

Introduction

This book is about the straight-forward truth regarding how to sell final expense with the added goal of making this information as actionable and relevant as possible to new and experienced final expense agents wanting to improve their craft

To be blunt, most of what you'll find on the web and from final expense "trainers" trying to sell you books, programs, and recruiting you is nothing more than fluff at best, and at worst, harmful to your final expense career.

My personal goal in my life as a salesperson, trainer, and agency is to eliminate bullshit and to speak the truth. My goal is to provide THE BEST resource for actionable, relevant, and real information on how to sell final expense compared to anything else.

Unlike many involved in the final expense business, I practice what I preach. Not only do I train my agents on the same material you are about to read in this book, but I also employ the same tactics and strategies in this book in my own personal business selling final expense insurance.

Unfortunately, much like the life insurance industry writ large, the final expense business is populated by what I call "marketers," who are great at recruiting warm bodies, but absolutely pathetic at both practicing what they preach. This is why **you must tread cautiously**

who you trust to teach you to sell final expense successfully.

I wish there were a book like mine when I first started. Many of the "marketers" teach final expense using a high-pressure, "used car salesman" type of approach, lying and deliberately misleading prospects while brow-beating prospects into policies. Just the other day, I was field-training a new agent who had originally kissed-off the idea of selling final expense because of a high-pressure trainer he trained with years ago who steam-rolled prospects into sales. Bad idea!

You can sell final expense in a low pressure and consultative manner, allowing you to sell ethically, make a good living and do right by your clients. This is exactly what I'm going to detail how to do in this book.

The way to read this book can be done front to back. You can also read particular sections based on how you want to digest the information.

The first part of this book will discuss some basics. For example, I'll discuss how to find the best final expense agencies to work for, what to look for analyzing final expense appointment contracts so you do not get taken advantage of. You will also learn how to quickly familiarize your carriers, what options you have regarding final expense leads.

The one point I will not push in this book is the "Drink the Kool-

Aid" kind of talk. I'm assuming you already have the guts and burning desire to succeed, before purchasing this book.

Once we talk about the basics of final expense, I'll delve into the actual sales presentation and prospecting method I teach all my new final expense agents. If you are new to selling final expense or looking for an actionable reference on how top producers sell, you'll get a boatload of value out of this section.

Shameless plug alert! If you read this book and are interested in working with me, feel free to visit my website at http://www.FEAgentMentor.com for more information on my Mentorship Program.

Who should read this book?

The first group of agents who should read my book are agents interested in selling final expense that are not already.

This includes people who considering getting licensed. Maybe they're not sure if the final expense business can be profitable or if it is fun (yes it is, well, most of the time!), and want to get an idea of how it's sold and want an honest perspective about how selling final expense really works. For potential final expense agents looking for a realistic diatribe on how this particular business works, you will find this book immediately applicable.

The second group who should read my book consists of currently-licensed agents who have done some life insurance sales but are curious to see how the final expense business works. Truth be told, much of selling final expense life insurance is similar to effectively selling traditional life products. However, you'll learn the small nuances of final expense you otherwise wouldn't learn off the cuff on your own through reading this book.

The third group who should read my book are final expense agents already selling final expense on a regular basis. If you are relatively new and have little to no access to quality field training, this book is for you.

Lastly, let's talk about who should not read this book. First of all, if you're looking for some sort of spiritual awakening or rah-rah motivational material, don't buy this book. Doing my research in preparation to publish my book, I reviewed much of my competition's books and training material, and much of it is perfect for those looking for pep-talks, motivational speeches, and getting drunk on the Kool-Aid. If you are looking for that, save your money. Don't buy my book.

Why Listen to David?

First of all, maybe you shouldn't listen to me. I don't know. And to help you figure that out, all I can do is share my story in the final expense business and let you decide if my experience is worthwhile to helping advance your skill-set and career.

First of all, I would be a liar if I told you I've only experienced incredible, exponential success, year over year without concern or stress. My career in final expense has been speckled, filled with ups and downs. Allow me to explain.

My first year in the business I experienced great success as a new agent. However, due in part to my own failures, I temporarily quit shortly after my first twelve months in the business. Convincing myself that I could create an edge with a totally new (and completely unproven) marketing approach, I diverted my focus away from the fundamentals of selling final expense, ultimately forcing me to go to work for someone else to make ends meet.

Luckily, while working full-time in a corporate sales position, I was able to refocus on the core fundamentals of final expense on a part-time basis, eventually breaking free of "working for the Man," and going solo after spending the prior year getting back on my feet.

After some time had passed, I decided my ups and downs in the business allowed me the capability to both recruit and train final expense agents on how to be successful. That's when I started my national agency Final Expense Agent Mentor, where I train agents on how to succeed in the final expense business.

As of 2016, this is my fifth year exclusively focusing on selling final expense. In 2015, I had my best year ever as both a producer and operator of Final Expense Agent Mentor, personally selling over 450 applications and having trained close to 200 final expense agents.

I share this experience with you not to brag, but to convey that my perspective on how to really, truly succeed in final expense is based on being both at the top of my game as well as in the deepest lows of failure. When agents work with me or read my training material, I make an active effort to help them understand what they are studying does NOT come from an agent who's had an extended period of luck, but has come from someone who has gone through both thick and thin.

Personally, I think this differentiating point is paramount to understand because much of sales is taught by those who CAN'T sell, just like much of how final expense is taught by people who CAN'T or DON'T sell final expense. You don't want to take their advice if you are serious about long-term success in this field.

Another reason you may want to consider listening to what I have to say is because, **well, most final expense training sucks.**

Talking to countless agents, it becomes obvious that final expense is run mostly like a multi-level marketing scheme. It's all about recruiting, never about teaching agents on how to sell a lot of burial insurance.

And what little training you do get amounts to throwing a brochure at you and kicking you out the door to fend for yourself. Now there's nothing wrong with that at a certain point. A lot of learning final expense is about DOING final expense. Unfortunately, many agencies don't have successful producers or "trainers" with more than a few months in the business. A few months in business is simply not enough time to fluently understand - much less teach - how to sell final expense consistently and successfully.

The concept of the way that I train agents how to sell is based on selling the best quality of business so that your business has the best chance of not only paying you the most but staying on the books for the longest possible time. Most final expense training approaches focus on steam-rolling prospects into sales, relying on high-pressure sales tactics, or teaching agents that you have to expect to rebuttal objections, at least five times before wearing the prospect out enough to convince them to buy.

Beyond feeling like a goober, here's the problem selling like this, and what you'll never hear from trainers who teach like this. None of this business sticks!

I remember one story about a successful car salesman who got into final expense. He outsold most of his fellow agents and had the highest application volume for the year. However, along with is, high production came high cancelation rates. And within a year, he was back to selling cars because he could not keep up paying back advanced commission on canceled policies.

Why did this happen? Because every morning your prospect decides whether or not they want to keep or cancel the policy you sold them. And if they cancel early, you are potentially on the hook for paying back the advanced commission you were given.

There MUST be a thoughtful consideration in how you go about selling in this business, as the old saying goes, "the policy that pays is the policy that stays!"

Another factor you must consider is agents are usually on the short end of the stick relative to their agency. What do I mean? Agents are routinely short-changed and sold what I call "Blue Sky." In other words, they are sold a bunch of crap by an agency representative that doesn't ever pan out, and lo and behold, because of the new agent's lack of final expense experience. They lose because their agency contracts stifle their income-earning capability, or worse, actually legally "steal" their income if they leave the agency!

Look. Agents get screwed in this business and the odds are you've talked to a couple organizations that look at you like cattle fodder. It's a nasty reality of this business and few openly talk about it. This book will go into detail about what you need to look for when reading contracts, and what pros and cons to be aware of when you're looking to partner with a final expense agency.

What's fantastic about this book is that much of what you're going to learn are lessons no agency or agent will tell you. And by reading this book, you can prevent an early end to a once-promising career. Hopefully, combined with my experiences on my successes and failures, you'll find this book valuable as it will save you thousands, maybe even tens of thousands in lost commissions you otherwise would have lost working with an inadequate final expense organization.

Final Expense Agency Contract Scams - Learn How To Stay Away From The Worst Possible "Opportunities"

Every day, a bad final expense agency somewhere is screwing over a new agent. Misrepresentation and hype give the final expense industry a bad name, so much that many potential final expense agents wonder if selling final expense insurance really is a good career. The purpose of this section is to show you what to look out for regarding final expense agency contracts as a new final expense agent. Also, I will discuss the contracts agencies give you so that you are better informed when it comes to selecting the best sales opportunity for the short- and long-term of your career. Lastly, I will talk about how to make sure you're not getting involved in final expense relationships that are hazardous to your career.

This is the legal disclaimer: *I am only a final expense agent. The information provided is not intended to be consumed as legal counsel or advice but understand it is purely informational in scope. This is not designed to be specific legal counsel. This is just information; you use it to the extent that you feel necessary. Please consult a professional, licensed attorney for any questions regarding final expense agency contracts. Again, I am not a lawyer. I'm just an agency operator and a final expense agent expressing personal commentary about what I see wrong with how many a final expense agency will treat their agents.*

With the legal disclaimer behind us, let's get into the final expense agency contract discussion.

First of all, final expense agency contracts are used to reduce legal and financial risk exposure to the agency. Contracts are designed to protect both parties, and to expressly discuss the responsibilities of each party in the business relationship. It names specific rules of procedure so that there's no confusion about how the relationship is supposed to work.

Regarding final expense agency contracts, most are designed to give the agency extreme leverage over the agent. They're designed to penalize agents, and extract more control from the agent regarding commissions and business.

Final Expense Agency Scam #1 - Captive Agencies With Two-Year Vesting Clauses

Let's talk about some real-world final expense agency contracts to avoid. The first contract you'll see is regarding a very well-advertised, captive company. If you've done any due diligence regarding final expense agencies, you'll know exactly who I'm speaking about.

What we're going to talk about with this particular contract is what's called "vesting." Vesting to the nature of who owns your commissions and renewals made from selling.

With this captive company, they stipulate that vesting does

not occur until two years after the agency agreement is in effect. This contract further clarifies that compensation payable under the contract will be forfeit if the agency contract is not vested. What does all this legal mumbo jumbo mean? The takeaway point here is that if you terminate the contract or if you are terminated, that agency owns all future income to the company, **your future income becomes the company's.**

Here's some food for thought. What if you're terminated in month 23 of your final expense agency contract? You've got a lot of business on the books after 23 months; what happens to that commission that you haven't received yet? **The commissions and the renewals become the ownership of the agency.** And yes, you signed off on this. There's nothing that you can legally do.

What if you hate the final expense business? We all think we're going to get in this business and succeed. But many people just don't like it for whatever reason. What if you did 6 months and you hate it and you want to move on? What happens? You will be terminated. Your renewals and commissions you haven't received become the final expense agency's commissions.

Be careful as the biggest final expense agency scams will be legally "stealing" your hard work if you're not careful. Let's call it what it is, it is bullshit. Unlike agents that work for this company, independent agents are IMMEDIATELY vested. If you left an independent agency and did not sign off on vesting paperwork, your renewals come with you.

Most new agents don't have any idea about the subject of vesting. This is one of the biggest things that a big final expense agency will do to make the most money possible. In this company, it's the managers make the big money, not the agents, and pilfering agents' commissions and renewals is why.

Final Expense Agency Contract Scam #2 – "Very Popular, National Final Expense Agency"

Hopefully, you understand why I don't give out specific names of final expense agencies. However, if you've done any type of due diligence via Google, you've probably run across these guys. Just like most final expense agencies, these guys look great on the surface but have a number of festering issues beneath the surface designed to screw over agents.

Have you seen the movie Braveheart? In the movie, nobles would exact "jus primae noctis" on newly-married couples (I'll let you Google "jus primae noctis"). Jus primae noctis in the context of a final expense agency allows them to "own" you, preventing you from pursuing advantageous relationships outside of their influence.

Let's go into specifics. According to this particular final expense agency's producer contract you MUST sign to work with them, **if you terminate your final expense agency contract with this agency,**

you must return all leads and any referrals gained to the agency including from third-party associations like lead vendors that you paid FULL price for. While this may sound reasonable on the surface, this particular agency does NOT pay for your leads.

If they DID pay for your leads, then they own your leads. You should return them. The point here is that you pay for your leads full retail cost. They simply referred you to that lead relationship.

They're demanding that you have to send not just the leads, but also referrals that are generated by policy-holders who were sold policies through this particular agency. They claim legally they own BOTH your referrals and your leads, even though you paid full price for them. How stupid is that?

I will acknowledge that it's one thing to PUT silly language into a final expense agency contract. But would the company actually follow through? I can't say for certain. But the fact they're putting this restrictive garbage in a contract MEANS they have thought through ways to take legal action against agents.

Let's continue analyzing this final expense agency contract scam. Further investigation shows that agents may associate with other life insurance companies, ONLY with prior consent from the agency. And that's whether or NOT the current agency even OFFERS the carrier to contract with!

Simply put, you're a slave to this final expense agency. Let's say you find a great final expense carrier or even a great life insurance company to offer non-final expense products like term insurance. The problem still remains. You still have to get "permission" from this agency to run your business the way you want!

If you leave this final expense agency, you also agree not to associate with any current or past carriers the agency was associated for 1 year. **So, if you worked six months, then quit, not only are CURRENT relationships with carriers at jeopardy, the past relationships, even if this final expense agency currently doesn't DO business with them!**

If you decide to leave them, they own you for the next year on current and past relationships. The real kicker is this: how do you know who your former agency has had an association with? What if the agency does a bad job for you? Too bad. You're still screwed!

Hopefully, it is obvious how silly the restraints are in the individual final expense producer. But you cannot think, "Okay, it's just a contract, who cares? How would the final expense agency follow through on this?" Here's where it gets ugly.

The consequences of breaking these rules are that the final expense agency contract stipulates that all future commissions and renewals become the property of the agency.

For example, if you leave this final expense agency, associate with a former carrier the agency used to work with but does not currently, you're toast! If the final expense agency you left finds out, you have signed off saying that they have permission to take your commissions and renewals. When you come aboard, you are a captive agent to their final expense agency. They own you! And the sad thing is agency presents themselves as the "aw-shucks, family-oriented, religious piety" type of organization. But is that truly the case, after taking a hard look at how prohibitive and potentially- damaging the final expense agency contract can be?

It's actually very simple for this final expense agency to claim "breach of contract," and take your remaining first-year commissions and renewals as settlement. Every state's department of insurance publicly lists each licensed agent, and which carriers they are with.

These particular final expense agency contracts are so one-sided and designed to screw you as an agent. How can you trust these agencies?

The ideal situation is to only sign carrier contracting. Every carrier has a specific contract to sign. The contracts will stipulate commission levels, what will lead to termination, etc. When an agency provides their own contract in addition to the carrier contract, be worried about more disclaimers and contingencies. Most likely this means the agency is attempting to pull "gotcha clauses" on you to take away your hard-earned commissions.

That's how these final expense managers make a killing. **They**

take over renewal streams and commissions that were earned by the terminated agent. Remember the best final expense agency to get involved with is the one that has both short-term and long-term advantages. Get involved selling final expense with an agency focused on providing you the short-term advantage of training, but also the long-term ability to grow.

There are agencies like mine, at Final Expense Agent Mentor, where I don't have anybody sign a final expense agency contract above and beyond what the carrier signs. You know exactly how our relationship works, and how I deal with my agents. I want our relationship to be simple, straightforward and transparent with no bullshit!

My Favorite Final Expense Carriers As Of 2016

Whether your new or experienced, finding the best final expense carriers to sell for is critical to your short- and long-term survival as a final expense agent.

An agent selling final expense burial insurance has many options as to which final expense carriers to work with. Picking the best final expense carriers can be confusing and daunting. This chapter will identify the different paths a new final expense agent can take and to discuss the pros and cons of each, as well as reference some of my favorite final expense companies you can use.

Your first option is to work as a captive agent. This means you work exclusively with one agency and normally sell one final expense product. The benefit to the new agent is that it simplifies the process and keeps new agents accountable.

However, the downside to teaming up with a captive agency is that the reality of final expense is the best agents broker multiple final expense companies to give their clients the best coverage at the best prices. There is no one final expense company that works the best for every scenario. And force-fitting one product on everyone is a sure-fire way to get your policies replaced while simultaneously suffering charge-backs.

Another option for a new final expense agent is becoming an independent agent. An independent final expense agent typically has access to the same type of lead and sales programs a captive agent does but has the ability to contract with multiple final expense carriers. The cons of this approach are only short-term. The new final expense agent will have more carriers and information to learn versus the captive agent. However, the final expense agent representing multiple products will experience far greater ability to sell more business with a better ability to shop and underwrite with multiple final expense carriers.

The advice of many final expense agents is to gravitate towards becoming an independent agent as quickly as possible if they want to sustain success for the long-run. Much of the process of being overwhelmed can be managed if the agent works with a tenured and experienced managing agent. To lessen the burden of learning the final expense business, new independent agents are recommended to start with two or three core final expense companies, preferably that are easy to underwrite, simple to understand, and competitively-priced. A good final expense manager upline will help you find those easy-to-work-with final expense carriers, but as you grow you will need the ability to pick up more carriers to fit specific underwriting niches.

Lastly, make sure you work with an upline manager that understands the Final Expense Business. They will be your best bet to help you find final expense carriers that not only will simplify your life, but also allow you the most latitude to place the most final expense business.

Check out the links below to both videos and articles of my favorite final expense carriers:

United Heritage Final Expense Carrier: **An** excellent "all-around" best final expense carrier to work with. Competitive pricing, great commissions, and flexible underwriting. Agents who prefer working with one core carrier will LOVE United Heritage.

Aetna/American Continental Final Expense Company - Extremely flexible on heart and circulatory prescriptions, pays great commissions on both Graded and Level coverage. Aetna will cover healthy people up to age 89! Great carrier for niche health situations, too.

Standard Life And Casualty Final Expense Carrier - My favorite "price-buster" final expense company. Surprisingly flexible underwriting for a pricing model that virtually beats all other carrier options. Home office staff and underwriting are especially helpful.

Security National Life Final Expense Company - Great bread and butter carrier that ONLY does a prescription check (no MIB check). Very simple to write, great rates, and an extremely high issue-as-applied-for rate relative to other carriers. Also pays a 10% lead co-op bonus when you issue only 1000AP monthly.

Great Western Final Expense Carrier: One of few independent carriers that do not do a prescription check or an MIB check for Level coverage. Also has a competitively-priced guaranteed issue product. Although there are a few drawbacks, Great Western is a great niche product to have in your portfolio.

Royal Neighbors of America Final Expense Company: If you love paperless applications, you will love Royal Neighbors. Extremely flexible underwriting and decent pricing, very well niche carrier for those who hate paperwork.

Can A New Final Expense Agent Successfully Sell Part-Time?

I have found many agents interested in selling final but don't want to jump in and let go of their full-time position. I get asked a lot by a lot of agents, "Can you do final expense part-time basis?" I'll be the first person to tell you that *you absolutely can*! Many people will tell you that you need to "burn the bridge," meaning you've got to quit whatever you're doing and devote all your energy to final expense.

Now a couple of things about myself. I used to work at a uniform services company due to me initially failing at the final expense business. Basically, I had to get a corporate job with a guaranteed income. I wanted to sell final expense part time, but I had to give myself some breathing room to get back on my feet.

So I took this job, and decided to sell final expense part time but give final expense a 100% effort. Here's how I made it work:

1. I would go work 3 days of final expense in the field.

2. I'd start around 2 or 3 o'clock - I was able to hit my prospecting goals at my corporate job early enough with plenty of time to sell final expense part time.

As I was out in the field, even though I would sell final expense part time, I worked my butt off, staying out until 10 or 11 working appointments. I was completely dedicated to getting back on my feet and being successful at final expense, despite my initial failure because I didn't want to be stuck in the corporate world any longer than I already had been.

Even though I could see a potential career track working at my corporate job, it was clear that upward mobility is extremely limited in a corporate environment. There's much more politics, and your effort and capabilities are going to be stymied in many circumstances when you work for "the Man."

That's where even an opportunity to sell final expense part time is fantastic. You don't need anybody to tell you how hard or what your limitations are when you work, it's totally up to you.

The point here is that if you get involved with final expense. The important thing to understand is that you give it 100% effort, despite your time limitations and what that means is that you've got to get out there, you've got to door knock every single lead you see. If you need somebody to set appointments, find an appointment-setter to work the leads for you so you can be more efficient than going out directly to see the people cold, through a door knock. Make sure you stay committed to buying leads.

All the same behavior traits apply when learning to sell final expense part time as much as it is for full-time agents. I've got an agent up in Kentucky doing really great in this business. He's got a full-time position in another industry, and he is giving it 100% despite selling final expense part time.

When he's in the field, he's doing all the right things. He's consistent. He's getting in front of the people. And over time, as he develops his skill level and he develops confidence in return when he's ready to leave his position, he can jump in 100% full-time and make a heck of a lot of money.

In summary, as a new agent, if you're looking at the final expense business from the outside in, and you can find a way to dedicate even two to two and a half days a week in the field, you can make a success out of selling final expense part time if:

1) You commit yourself to the lead program,

2) You commit yourself to the process of learning this business over a 6 to 12 month period, and

3) You work with somebody who knows what they're doing and how to instruct and mentor you on actually succeeding in the final expense business.

A Primer On Prospecting For Final Expense

Prospecting is simply the act of finding people that have some marginal level of interest in your product or service. To clarify for folks new to sales, just because you have a prospect does not mean you have a buyer! However, it does mean that you have someone with "an open mind" to what you have to offer. **Finding a large number of people out with open minds to your offering is the cornerstone to success in this business.**

And the real component to long-term success is continual, non-stop prospecting in large numbers. Seeing and talking to as many people as possible about final expense life insurance, and asking all those people to do business with will cause you to realize massive results. That's where the majority of your success is going to come from, and my goal in this book is to show you the different ways to successfully prospect so as to help you determine what works best for you.

First, we will start with prospecting fundamentals.

As a life insurance agent, **your prospecting goal is to set an appointment**. It's that simple. No matter if you're prospecting in person or over the phone, your prospecting goal is to get a face to face appointment to discuss what you have to offer.

Throughout the first 12 months of my prospecting career, I went through a phase of wanting to "reinvent the wheel" regarding prospecting. I had experienced many times where I'd run an appointment and get stood up, or I'd run an appointment and dealt with an unqualified prospect. I would wonder, "Is it really wise to set an appointment without any facts or information? Or do you prospect, set an appointment, and pre-qualify entirely over the phone, to the point of knowing which plan to apply for and simply needing signatures?"

After having success with both methods, I determined for myself and through discussions with top gun final expense agents, that **simply asking for an appointment is the best method to sell the most life insurance.**

The takeaway here is this: simplicity works in this business. Just introduce yourself and who you are with, why you are dropping in in-person or calling over the phone, and then ask for the appointment. Besides handling a few basic knee-jerk objections, this is all you need to set good appointments to discuss final expense insurance.

The biggest difference between how I personally prospect, and how others prospect, is that **I recommend new final expense agents to prospect with warm leads versus cold calling**. I drop several thousand mail pieces and get response cards back that I set my appointments from. How I set lead card appointments compared to cold call appointments is exactly the same, with only a few minor exceptions.

The benefit of using warm leads is that prospecting time is vastly reduced, and you sit with more qualified prospects. And, to gain an even greater level of efficiency, much of what I've mentioned above can be outsourced to an appointment-setter, allowing you to see more people and sell more policies.

Let's discuss in detail each form of prospecting and lead generating, describing how the process works, what the pros and cons are, and give you a sample script as to how I would get in the door doing both.

Most of my final expense business has focused around prospecting warm leads over the phone and in person. However, I have done a significant amount of prospecting business-to-business. The truth is that prospecting in any industry is pretty much the same. It is simply a matter of (a) talking to a lot of people about your product or service, and (b) learning what knee-jerk objections you need to rebuttal, and always asking for the appointment, and lastly (c), which is developing your phone presence through tonality emphasis and word selection.

Let's first start by discussing cold calling over the telephone.

Cold calling over the phone is just like it describes; it's the act of picking up your phone and dialing somebody you've never talked before, and asking for an appointment to show them what you have to offer.

Through many discussions with final expense agents, **cold calling over the phone isn't the best use of your time.** The reason is that the Do Not Call List Registry is so tremendously large; many people who might be interested in your offering have opted out from receiving telemarketing solicitation. Plus, every residence heavily screens inbound calls with Caller-ID, voicemail setup, and is generally spiteful towards telemarketing of any kind.

If your only option is to prospect cold over the phone, the best way to use web-based software power dialer. Power dialers automate the dialing process so you can dial multiple lines simultaneously, thus talking to more people in less time. Auto-dialers allow you to leverage your time and dial up to, in some cases, three or even four lines at a time, with the anticipation that most aren't going to get through. However, you'll be able to talk to 25 to 40 people per hour and concentrate your efforts on generating qualified leads.

The benefit of using a dialer is talking to more people in less time. If you're skilled at setting appointments, you'll be able to get in front of a lot of people, meaning you'll sell more policies. Phoning is a different skill set than door-knocking; you must possess perseverance despite the sea of no's you will certainly experience. You must always be prepared to rebuttal against the typical knee-jerk objections you will face. And you must be cognizant of your voice tonality and how you convey the message you've prepared.

Besides the action of cold calling on the phone, **the best way to develop your phone skill is to practice your pitch in front of a loved one or to record your voice live on the phone with a prospect.** Both methods allow for immediate feedback and course-correction. Hopefully, your spouse will give you constructive criticism on how you sound, and you can learn tons you otherwise would miss by listening to a recorded live call to a prospect.

What should you look for when you listen to your recording? Take note of filler language you use like, "Uhh," "Uhmm, "Uh ya okay." This language conveys nothing to your prospect at best and shows you to be unprofessional at worst. Also, note how well you pace your speaking. If you have prospects saying, "Huh?", "What did you say?" then you're probably talking too fast. Also, are you adjusting your pace and tonality to emphasize the most important points?

Another benefit to dialing is how little it cost. If you can invest $100 to $150 a month and have an internet connection and a computer, you'll be able to have full access to the best power-dialer options on the market.

Now let's discuss the drawbacks of using the dialer as your primary prospecting tool. First, with limited residences to call on, you will face larger drive times to see your prospects. More drive time equals less opportunity to present. Second, you will spend a lot more time working the telephone to set appointments; there's no way around that. You're going to be on the phone a lot more, meaning less time selling in person.

Typically for cold callers, you will have a lower ceiling to the maximum number of appointments you can set, simply because one must invest at minimum 10 to 15 hours a week telemarketing to fill up that number of appointments. More so, as a rule of thumb, appointments need to be set for the next day at best, two days out at worst, as no-show rate increase as each day passes. So it is imperative you spend the day before your day in the field on the phone setting appointments.

A lot of folks new to cold prospecting on the phone wonder how long it takes to set an appointment. First of all, your skill to set appointments develops over time; as you develop your skill, you'll begin to set more appointments with less work. However, results wax and wane; sometimes it'll only take an hour to set up your day, other times you'll call for 4 or 5 hours and nobody wants to see you. Beyond the importance your phone skill, your results are tied directly to the total calls you make.

In my business-to-business experience cold prospecting over the phone, it took an hour on average to set one appointment. As I described above, there were days I could set five appointments in 30 minutes; other days it would take calling all day to set one. More likely than not, it will take an hour to two hours before you set an appointment. As you get better, you will set more appointments in fewer calls – but as a new agent expect to invest a minimum of 15 hours prospecting at different times during the day to fully book your field day.

Now, let's discuss what to say on the phone when you talk to a live person about final expense life insurance. The script I am providing comes from personal experience, heavily prospecting cold as a business-to-business salesman.

Your approach is simple; **sell the appointment, not the product.** The less you say the better. Getting into too much detail will give the prospect a reason not to see you. Focus on sounding exciting. Focus on sounding legitimate. Establish this aura within the first few seconds as you go through the script, then confidently ask for the appointment, and prepare to rebuttal any knee-jerk objections that arise.

So here's my script whenever I pick up the phone and make cold calls:

Prospect answers: "Hello?"

You say: *"Hi, this is Mrs. Jones, right?"* (Asking this way communicates that you know her name and might be familiar, thus many people relax a little and are engaged when asked this way. Also, you will have this information when you purchase your cold calling list.)

Prospect: "Yes, who is this?"

You say: (Introduction): *"Hi Mrs. Jones, This is David Duford with Tennessee Senior Benefits."* **The Introduction is a way to clearly designate who you are and with whom you work for. Providing your business name will establish a base level of credibility.**

You say: (Purpose of Call) *"Mrs. Jones, the reason I'm calling is I help seniors age 60 and older find affordable, state-regulated final expense life insurance that helps people like you pay for burial costs in an affordable manner."*

Or I may say something like, *"Mrs. Levine, this is David Duford from Tennessee Senior Benefits. Hey, the reason I'm calling you is that I work with folks like you who are looking for an affordable way to pay for final expenses with a state-regulated burial insurance program."*

Stating the purpose of the call is vital. You must tell them why you are calling and tie in a possible benefit to the prospect for the purpose. In the script above, I pointed out "affordable" as the benefit. You could go point out an emotional benefit. *"I help seniors in Tennessee relieve the burden of paying for final expenses like burial cost and cremation with affordable, state-regulated final expense plans."* You want to hit on one benefit, as the longer the spiel with more benefit statements added, you'll lose their engagement.

You: (Appointment Close): *"I'm the agent in Bradley County that helps people out with these programs, and I need 10 minutes of your time to show you how these programs work. Would Tuesday, tomorrow, at 10:00 or 2:00 work best for you?"*

In the appointment close, it's important you stress it is your job to help this prospect out, and you emphasize brevity of the appointment, while also expressing control through "needing" 10 minutes. Lastly, you conclude every Appointment Close with a closing statement assuming the appointment, but asking for a selection of a preferred time.

The reason why this appointment-setting script works is that it conveys trust, a possible benefit to the prospect, and you are assuming the appointment.

Naturally, some will object to your appointment. Below are some of the typical objections you will hear, along with the appropriate rebuttals:

"I've got enough life insurance." "What is this about?"

"Send me something in the mail," "I've already got an agent." "Never call me again."

As a cold prospector, you have to understand the nature of cold calling. You are using an interruptive prospecting medium. You'll talk to people who are engaged in other activities when you begin to pitch them; that is why you often hear objections. They are not entirely engaged, thus they may not have totally thought through what you are offering. While not every rebuttal will result in a sale or appointment, rebuttals force your prospect to re-engage and reevaluate.

Be prepared to handle these typical objections, and understand if you get initial resistance that the person over the phone isn't necessarily uninterested. It's natural to resist salespeople, so the stronger the rebuttal, the more appointments you'll set and the more you'll sell.

The most common objection you'll hear is, "Oh, I've already got life insurance." Don't be dissuaded by this. The phrase "Life Insurance" means different things to different people. For some, it means a term policy on their house. For others, it's burial insurance. And others yet it is income replacement. The point is you don't know what they mean by life insurance, so you have to accept their rebuttal and describe to them briefly how this is entirely different.

What I say to the "Already have life insurance" rebuttal is this:

"That's okay, Mrs. Jones. Most people I talk to already have life insurance and the reason they meet with me anyway is my program can improve on what they have either with better pricing or better coverage. I need 10 minutes of your time, and what you do with this information is totally up to you. Did you think that 10:00 or 2:00 would work better for you tomorrow?"

Let me go into detail about this rebuttal, as the framework of every rebuttal is virtually the same.

First, I agree with the perspective of the prospect. I emphasize, not fight; I might even stroke her ego for the decision regarding life insurance she made. So I'm going to say, "I understand, Mrs. Prospect," or "That's totally fine, Mr. Prospect!" Then I'm going to provide some third-party evidence that this is what most people say when I call. This is supposed to hopefully engender a modicum of trust as well as perk up some curiosity.

Second, I pique their curiosity. Next I say, "The reason people meet with me anyway is a lot of the times, I'm able to show them how to get more coverage or pay less for what they have and really just give them more value." After I've previously put them at ease and perked the curiosity, I give them a benefit statement that may interest her.

Third, I SELL the appointment: "Mrs. Jones, all I need is a quick 10 minutes to show you what this is like in person, and what you do with it is totally up to you." I say that to relieve them that I'm not there to sell them or push them around; what they do with the information is up to them! You're not obligated whatsoever to do anything, but at least, you'll have facts. And then I close for the appointment: "Is Thursday at 2:00 or 10:00 better for you?"

So here is the basis of every rebuttal: Emphasize, Benefit,

Close. Recapping, I validated their objection, told them why there's still benefit in a meeting, then I soft-closed for a brief, informational, no-stress appointment. This rebuttal approach engages the suspect, gets them to reconsider, and hopefully more often than not, agree to an appointment.

Now, it's very probable you'll get an objection to your rebuttal. For example, say you replied to the objection exactly as stated above, and the suspect says, "Listen, I'm just not interested. I appreciate your time," then feel free to hang up. At least, you tried! I personally do not believe you should not worry about hard-rebuttals, as it can become demoralizing as a new agent with people yelling at you, or hanging up rudely on you. No body's going to come unhinged with a single rebuttal, and more often than not, you'll get an appointment out of the attempt.

However, a lot of times your rebuttal to the initial objection will get a "softer" objection. It's not really an objection, more like a question. Examples like, "What kind of program is this" or "How much does it cost?"

These are "buying questions," indicating interest in your product. These are the type of objections you want to turn around and close on. Use the same rebuttal framework, "*Mrs. Jones, that's a great question! I have over 30 programs available, and to figure out which one works best, I'm required to stop in for 10 minutes and ask you a few questions – again, there's no obligation, and whatever you do with the info is totally up to you! How's Tuesday at 5 sound?*"

(Emphasize, Benefit, Close).

You'll get other rebuttals, such as, "Okay, can you just send me some information in the mail?" Your reply, "No, my boss requires me to show you this in person. What you do with it is up to you, Mrs. Jones. If you like it, great; if not, no hard feelings. Does that sound fair?"

This rebuttal works because you place blame elsewhere; you say no and blame it on somebody else. It shows her you're not pushy and you're just trying to do your job right.

And then you go into selling the appointment. *"All I need is 10 minutes, Mrs. Jones. Whatever you do, like I said, what you do with it's up to you. If you like it, great; if not, you're not going to hurt my feelings. I'm not there to hard sell you. Is that fair enough*?" You're just coming to terms and being frank with them, but being diplomatic. And then you close for the appointment.

Other things you'll hear are "I'm busy today; can you call back in a couple days?" This one can be a true. It's a matter of working around that. What you say is *"Okay, Mrs. Jones, you probably have a pretty busy day tomorrow. What you got going on?"* "Well, I've got to go to the doctor's and I've got to go to the grocery store tomorrow after that." *"What time, Mrs. Jones, do you expect to be home?"* "I don't really know." *"Mrs. Jones, if I put you down tentatively for 6:00, do you see any reason why that would be a problem?"*

What you're working on is because you've given them two times to work with, which in their mind, neither works well. So they'll just respond quickly to try to get you off the phone. If you respond back the way I described above suggest another time, "How about 6:00? Do you see any reason where you'd be tied up?"

And then if they give you a little more resistance, "Yeah, but can you send it in the mail?" just go into the same rebuttal. If they give any kind of resistance, just sell the 10 minutes. *"I just need 10 minutes, Mrs. Jones. What you do with it's up to you. Fair enough?"*

And then close for 6:00. *"Fair enough? Is 6:00 okay? Perfect."*

Those are the objections you will hear 95% of the time. You'll hear strange ones like "I'm already a life insurance agent." Well, okay, click! "I don't believe in life insurance." Alright, bye! You will hear all sorts of rebuttals that are crazy like that, but the vast majority of the ones are going to be "I've already got enough life insurance, I've already got enough burial insurance," "Can you send me something in the mail?" or "I'm busy."

There are several key tactics to use when setting the appointment. Number one, do not give your number out. You don't want to give them your number so they can call and cancel on you. Have the caller ID on your power-dialer show another number than your cell phone; I know some agents who use their fax numbers.

Number two, when you set the appointment, confirm the

address that you have on your list and ask them "Tell me specifically where your house is and what it looks like, any markers or anything." Get them engaged in the appointment process improves the odds they won't forget about you. Then once you do that, reconfirm the appointment, ask them to put it on their calendar, and tell them, "I'll see you tomorrow at 2:00, Mrs. Jones. I appreciate it" and get off the phone. It's that easy.

Your goal as a full-time agent should be 15 appointments a week.

A good rule of thumb is most agents sell half the final expense appointments they set. It is inevitable that some of the ones you set will no-show or cancel. If you end up setting 15, three or four shoo you away and you close the other half, if you're closing five deals a week without really any lead cost beyond gas and a dialer, that's incredible!

How To Prospect Cold Using
Face-To-Face Door Knocking

Door-knocking cold is the act of taking a list of suspects, and personally visiting each completely cold, in the hope of getting an appointment on the spot, or at a later date, to discuss your offerings.

When it comes to the final expense business, **my assessment is door-knocking a slightly more profitable prospecting method compared to cold phone calling,** because it's harder to be rude or dismissive of a real live person in front of you, plus suspects typically are more willing to give you a minute to explain what you have to offer out of courtesy.

Let's get into the dynamics of a cold door-knocking campaign. First, you need a list of people to see. I recommend starting with a list of 500 or 1000 people ages 50-80, with an income of less than $50,000. Ideally, buy a list in a blue collar neighborhood, or a small country town. Next, make the cold canvassing process efficient, use mapping software to plot a course, so you are not driving around in circles all day.

Now let's take you through the steps you'll take to effectively canvass your first prospect. Always park your car in the driveway of the prospect. I always suggest that you leave the door as you approach the door. The reason you do this is to appear from someone peeking out the window that you're not planning an extended visit; prospects are more likely to open the door if it looks like you'll be brief.

Make sure you carry a sample lead card to the door, along with a clipboard and your lead list you can take notes on. The lead card is used as a visual reference and a great "reason why" you're there in the first place. Seniors across the nation get many of these business reply mailers weekly. So what you're showing them will be somewhat familiar, and you can leverage these cards to your advantage to build a base level of legitimacy.

When you finally make it to the front door, knock on the door seven to nine times, hard. Now, don't beat the door down, but knock firm enough to be heard no matter where the prospect is in the house. Once you knock, I take a step back, giving, at least, three to five feet between me and the door. Whatever I do, I do not want to convey intimidation. I'm 6 foot tall, so stepping down a stair until they answer the doors shows I'm there in peace and not to get in their face.

As you wait, look into the peephole and smile, so when they peep out they'll see you looking at them, and they'll know that somebody's looking at them. This increases your odds at them opening the door.

When the suspect opens the door, they'll say "Hello," and I reply,

***"Hi, are you, Mrs. Joanne Smith*?"** You'll know their name because you have the prospecting list, and then she'll probably say, "Well, it depends. What can I do for you?" This is where you hand them a laminated card, maybe the sample you receive, and what you say is *"Hey Mrs. Jones, my name is David Duford. I'm with Tennessee Senior Benefits, and the reason I'm stopping by today"* – this is where you hand them the card – *"is that I help people like yourself, people over 50, find ways to relieve the burden of burial costs or final expenses with final expense state-regulated life insurance program.*

"I'm the agent in the area, and my job is to go out and visit people that we send these cards to. I'm sure you've gotten a lot of them in the mail. I wanted to see if you have 10 minutes for me to stop by now to show you how these programs work." With the cold canvass approach, you're asking for the appointment immediately versus setting it up for the following day as with cold calling over the phone. That's the main difference with working the door, is that your primary goal is getting into an appointment immediately.

Many times your prospects let you in before you even finish your approach; that's nice when that happens. Other times, you'll get similar rebuttals in person as you would over the phone. However, the big difference is that many people are more forthcoming about giving you information in person about their coverage versus over the phone. Over time, once you have a strong understanding of the competition and how their plans work, you will close many deals this way that you otherwise wouldn't with any other marketing method.

Of course, you'll hear objections, all of which are the same as cold calling over the phone. Handle the objections the same was as listed in the cold calling section, with the only slight change of asking for the appointment now if they haven't referenced the time being bad. The same appointment-setting rules apply for cold canvassing; resist the urge to book multiple days out, because you'll get no-showed in the same frequency as telephone-set appointments. As a cold canvasser, you do have the unique ability to apply body language in addition to your word choice. So make sure you make eye contact, smile, and dress professionally.

What kind of activity do you need to do to make cold canvassing successful? Focus getting at least 20, if not 30 door knocks in a day. And that means hit that number every single day, whether or not you have appointments pre-set. Consistently canvassing 30 doors a day is enough to get 3 to 5 appointments daily, and around 15 appointments a week. I do not recommend door knocking at 9:00 am. 10:00 am is the earliest I'd ever consider canvassing residentially. 11:00 am is a perfect time to begin canvassing. And don't stop canvassing until the sun goes down.

A couple of final pointers: for total disclosure, I've never cold canvassed for life insurance business. However, I have cold prospecting a ton in my former B2B position. Successful cold canvassers always recommend looking for visible signs the prospect is home – look for vehicles in the driveway, lights on, doors open, shades pulled open. Make sure to check with county and city guidelines on soliciting residential areas. Some charge you a daily or weekly fee to do so and other municipalities decide your state insurance license is enough to allow you to solicit.

Personally, in my city, you can carry your license and that will be an acceptable form of prospecting. Some agents – and I'm not making a recommendation, but what I've heard some agents doing -- is they quickly move from area to area without staying long enough to incur a fee. Consult your county government or city government to see what that is exactly. Make sure that you're on top of that so you don't get in trouble.

If you're making phone calls, go to www.InfoFree.com. You can get a monthly membership with all the data you need for a small fee. Combined with your auto-dialer, that's $200 a month for expenses and gas and all. You have monthly access to 5,000 to 10,000 names you can plug into your dialer. That's more than enough people to talk to each month.

If you're cold canvassing, use www.InfoFree.com for a list. Make sure you don't pick wealthy areas and dirt-poor areas to prospect. Really stick to more middle class, lower class neighborhoods that you feel comfortable knocking in. Pick out 150 names to work a week; maybe 200 to 250, and just go see them in person. A final point about all cold canvassing: **The reason I don't cold canvass is the process**

for me is emotionally draining. Getting rejected a lot takes it out of me, as well as for most cold callers. For me, using warm lead generation takes away most of the fear. I feel like they're calling on me versus the opposite, which changes your attitude and perspective about prospecting. Bottom line, you will get results with any cold prospecting system, as long as you commit yourself to the process.

Give yourself time to learn how to cold call. Most importantly, connect and work with an agent that can show you how on a first-hand basis. No, it doesn't come naturally for most, but it takes a unique skill set and resilient attitude to do it. Once you get good, setting appointments becomes fun because you're not going to have the lead expense like most agents do. All it is, it would be $200 bucks a month, and then anything else you make is all gravy. Selling four or five policies a week, an average $600 commissions, we're talking $12,000 a month before expenses – which expenses will be, after gas cost, probably are going to keep you above $11,000 net, and that's excellent, even on four or five policies a week selling final expense life insurance cold calling methods.

Using Warm Leads To Prospect

An Upfront Note: The script over the phone and in person for warm calling methods is generally the same. I'm going to spend less time on the actual scripts, because there are a lot of similarities, and devote more time on the different means and methods to generate warm leads. The most successful agents in the final expense business generate leads via direct mail business reply cards.

Very few final expense agents' cold prospecting for leads. In fact, ninety-nine percent of all agents are using leads to prospect. And virtually ALL top agents are using final expense direct mail leads to maximize their high level of production. In this chapter, we will discuss why an agent should use final expense direct mail leads. Including what the pros and the cons are of a final expense direct mail program.

So what is exactly direct mail as it relates to final expense? When we look around and talk to different agents and what they use, as far as a final expense lead program, almost all of them are doing what's called 'business reply mailers'. Business reply mailers are when a mail house mails out a mailer with detachable letters. The recipient can detach it, fill it out, throw it back in the mailbox. Eventually, about five weeks later, the agent gets the mail piece back.

Why do we use business reply mailers? And why are they a good source of final expense direct mail leads to begin with? First of all, a direct mail business reply card has one powerful advantage over all the other direct mail and all the other lead pieces of any kind, and that is **engagement.**

What I mean by that is when you look at one of these final expense lead cards is that the applicant actually fills out their information. They leave their name. They leave their address. Sometimes they leave their birthday. And sometimes even their email. Doing all this gets them more involved in the lead generation process. They look at the card. They think about it. They talk to and show the final expense lead card to their spouse. They eventually they fill it out, walk down to the mailbox, put it back in and boom-- that becomes a lead. So that process of higher engagement actually means that they're of better quality because **they're taken the time to really think about why and what this is and possibly seeing if they can do something about getting a plan to cover for final expenses.**

Let's talk about cons of the final expense direct mail lead. The con is that the price point is higher. But when it comes to any kind of lead, you get what you pay for. The higher the price, generally speaking, the higher the quality. So with final expense direct mail this is why you see the top 10% of agents using direct mail, because the lead is of higher quality, thus is more consistent and usually results in more frequent sales.

Some other advantages include when you use direct mail you have no 'do not call' solicitation restrictions. You can stay consolidated in an area pretty well. You don't have to worry about traveling 150 to 200 miles to stay busy like you would with telemarketing leads. Many agents in suburban metro markets can remain consolidated within a reasonable geographical area. Other cons to final expense direct mail leads: it's about a three or four or five week turnaround time to get leads. Also, you must buy a continual flow of final expense direct mail leads to make your lead flow consistently. That requires money and consistency of investment on a weekly basis.

For final expense agents starting out with minimal capital reserves to invest in a final expense direct mail lead program, direct mail is probably not for you. You're going to have to look at other things like telemarketing and cold calling to get yourself properly bankrolled to buy direct mail leads. Response rates for direct mail are continuing to go down. I've been in this business nearly five years. This business model is very attractive to a lot of people from different lines of insurance. You even see agents starting to sell final expense from entirely different industries. And with more agents dropping final expense mailers this reduces response rates, driving lead prices up.

I recommend for most final expense agents do some kind of fixed-price final expense direct mail leads program. That's where a mail house that has economies of scale that can drop hundreds of thousands of mail pieces, making money on volume, and passing the savings along to the agent.

Most of my agents do a fixed-price program, giving them the guarantee that their price point is never going to get higher and gets them in front of people that want life insurance. Not every final expense direct mail leads piece is perfect or not every lead program is perfect. But with direct mail and fixing your prices, it's a pretty good deal. Just make sure you know which final expense mailer is the best to use.

If you really are serious about final expense sales, the odds of you getting and needing to get involved in final expense direct mail are pretty high. The capital requirement is higher, but the quality makes up for all the higher investment.

Lastly An Important Overview Of What A Lead Really Is

First of all, let's define what a lead is. **A lead is nothing more than an individual who raises his hand and expresses a marginal level of interest in whatever it is that you are soliciting.**

A lead is not a guaranteed sale. Most leads don't throw their checkbook at you, ready to buy the moment you walk in. *They need to be sold!* They need somebody to convince them of what it is that they are interested in as something that they should buy. It is important to understand this difference because **when you are buying leads, you**

are not buying guarantees; you are buying opportunities. It is up to you to make those leads worth working.

Aged Final Expense Leads - Are They Worth It?

The topic of aged final expense leads is something that comes up from time to time. The biggest reason why is due to new agents having financial constraints on buying fresh direct mail leads or telemarketing leads.

Sometimes as a compromise, buying final expense aged leads is a good idea. And the purpose of this section is to discuss where you can find final expense aged leads, how to analyze if they are worth purchasing, what circumstances use aged leads, and what kind of sales results you can expect from them. Final expense aged leads are usually something that most marketing organizations or agencies will offer. You have larger agencies that have an inventory of final expense aged leads that are anywhere from several months old to several years old. Some of these leads are either worked or unworked.

Why would an agent want to use aged final expense leads?

The primary reason an agent uses aged leads is because it's a cheap way to get started. However, just as true as it is everywhere else in life, you get what you pay for. With aged leads comes a poorer quality lead. Aged final expense leads that are a year old or more will result in many of them that are dead, have moved, phones have been shut off because their Obamacare minutes are gone.

To most efficiently work your final expense aged leads, you

need to give maximal effort in door knocking them, plus you have to buy a mass load of them to get the best use out of them.

If you are desperate to get involved in selling final expense, and can string together enough money for final expense aged leads, I say go for it. However, you have to keep your expectations in line with what you're paying for; if you pay $100 for 50 aged leads and you sell 2 policies of them, then that's a great 10:1 return on your investment. You've got to go work them hard. You've got to buy a high volume of them. And you should treat working aged leads as a way to "step up" to bankrolling your eventual fresh direct mail lead program.

The Cost Of "Free"
Final Expense Leads

There are a lot of new final expense agents that "don't know what they don't know." Many final expense agencies offer free lead programs, and the agents think, "I just take these leads, I go out there and work, I make money."

Getting involved in the final expense business REQUIRES you to view your role as a business person. Every single business has some kind of operating cost. Businesses have costs of goods, raw materials, etc. Most businesses have to invest their money into something, before realizing a profit on selling the good.

In final expense, at least for brand new agents, that cost of goods sold is tied up in the marketing and lead investment portion of the business. It takes a solid $3,000 to $5,000 if you do it the right way with direct mail final expense leads. But a lot of agents don't have that getting started. If I run across a final expense agent who is flat broke and has an indomitable desire to succeed, I will recommend a final expense company that will provide free final expense leads. However, there are long-term consequences shacking up with an agency providing free leads in many cases -- very commonly they will NOT allow you to increase your commissions and build you up into a self-sufficient final expense agent paying for his own leads.

In truth, it's better for a final expense agent to work a weekend job, or work extra hours at the full-time job to bankroll their final expense lead program. This is truly how to start selling final expense the right way. But let's take a look at the long run and why free final expense leads are problematic:

1) There Is No such Thing As A Free Lunch. Somebody has to pay for your free final expense leads. And if you're not paying, then your agency is. I can guarantee they want to make a sizeable profit on your work given the risk they are taking providing you free final expense leads.

Here's how they do it. As a new final expense agent, you're going to start between 80% and 100% contracts in most organizations. This assumes your agency is willing to help develop, train, and support you in becoming a competent and independent final expense agent.

With the agencies providing free final expense leads, you'll start between a 45 to a 55% commission level. Your income-earning capability is cut in half.

Let's crunch numbers to see if this proposition makes sense.

First, take a guy doing $15,000 in issue paid business a month. This is what I would call a top 10% agent. He's getting free final expense leads. He's on a 50% contract, so he's making $7,500 before minor expenses like gas, wear and tear on his vehicle, etc.

Now let's look at an agent with 100% contract. He's doing $15,000 as well. And he's paying for his own leads.

As an aside, an agent paying for his own leads AND producing 15,000 in business most likely will be making between 110% to 120% average first year commissions, but I want to use 100% commissions as a conservative example.

When you consider final expense lead expenses, let's say he's needs 25 leads a week. Twenty-five leads a week at $30 each lead is $750 a week in lead spend. That's $3,000 a month. $15,000 in gross commission minus $3,000 in lead spend gives this agent $9,000 in net income. Comparing each agent, the agent paying for his own leads makes an additional $1,500 a month in net income, or an additional $18,000 a year. That's much better!

But wait, there's more. The renewal difference between free final expense lead providers and agents who buy their own leads is dramatic. Many times, **agents getting free final expense leads do NOT have renewals.**

The agent at a higher contract paying for his own final expense leads will have an approximate renewals commission of about 5%. Doing the math, $180,000 gross annual commission multiplied by 5% is around $9,000 in additional annual income! Nine-thousand dollars in annual renewal commission compared to zero renewal commission is a big difference, don't you think?

Apparently, agencies providing free leads want to manage their risk in buying leads for their agents, but where they make the big bucks is on getting the renewal commission. Over time, an agent receiving free final expense leads is leaving mid-five figures on the table. And we're only talking about renewals, not first-year commissions!

The idea of managing a final expense lead program is not complicated. It's simple once you get the hang of it.

In the beginning, you have to give up some first-year commission to be trained properly in this business. But when you turn into a top 10% final expense agent, agencies should be bending over backward to earn your business. So getting paid what you are worth should be easy to get at this point.

The important takeaway is to ensure you're getting value out of your final expense relationship. So if you're in this position, is it worth having free final expense leads over the long run? Compare your production numbers to 100% or even 110% contract to be safe. You'll be amazed at how much you're leaving on the table.

Final Expense Avatar
Telemarketing Leads

Telemarketing final expense leads involve a person calling a prospect or a name on a list and then qualifying them into a lead. Most telemarketing leads are just that; they're leads; they're somebody to talk to that has expressed a marginal level of interest in a life insurance product. Most of these leads are generated either by foreigners or by Americans and what I have found is that there are really two main kinds of final expense leads. They're either inexpensive and horrible quality, or they're expensive with "okay" quality and are very hard to come by, but before the illegalization of "robo-calls", getting a cheap, consistent source of telemarketing leads has been pretty tough to come by.

To give you some background, robo-calls were the software-generated calling that would call a thousand lines a minute and play a pre-recorded message upon picking up the phone. These were all over the market back in the 2000 to 2010 era of telemarketing but have pretty much altogether disappeared by now, except for those operations that still use them and want to take the risk of getting sued. The bottom line is that the robo-calls shut down a lot of the viability of telemarketing leads until this new advent of the great telemarketing known as avatar leads.

What are final expense avatar leads? How is this any different from any other final expense lead that's out there or any other lead in general?

Final expense avatar leads are mainly pre-recorded openings, closings and rebuttals recorded by an American English-speaking telemarketer or a professional voice over actor, but use recorded messages uploaded into a soundboard that's operated by a foreigner.

When the callers enter a conversation with a prospect, instead of the Filipino talking, he presses buttons on the pre-recorded soundboard with each comment and enters into a conversation to generate a lead. Why are final expense avatar leads a great lead to sell final expense to? The avatar lead delivers the same pitch with the same enthusiasm at all times and never gets discouraged. Think about it this way: we are human and there is variability that we are going to experience; some days are better than others.

You may be discouraged, you may have gotten into a fight with your wife if you're a telemarketer and that may dampen your effect and your ability to persuade somebody to agree to give information. This doesn't happen with final expense avatar leads. It is a terminator lead, it is a terminator telemarketer. He never wanes in his delivery and he converts more because of that. What happens is there are more leads that come out of this because it's the same strong delivery every single time and that's why the combination of using a low-cost foreign call center with persistent, unrelenting telemarketers is what allows us to generate quality leads at a low price.

What kind of expectations can you get from these final expense avatar leads? Here's my experience: I've worked these leads on a continual basis, I have agents that work these on a continual basis and usually these leads fall into one or two categories.

They're either gold or they're complete crap. There's not a lot of middle ground. The closing ratios tend to be lower than direct mail for most salesman, but the thing is because the lead price point is so low, the return on investment tends to be the same, if not higher, than what you would find in other regards.

For example, my expectation is if we can buy 30 of these leads and we can sell 10 to 20%, somewhere between 3 and 5 applications off of every 30 ordered, and you work hard, you can get that and that's going to be a 5:10 to 10:1 return on your lead investment. That's fantastic! Even though you're not closing a lot as a percentage of the leads, who cares? You're going to bank a lot because you're looking for the diamond in the rough; you're just looking for those 3 to 5 deals out of every 30 that are really good and who cares about the rest, even if they all were just horrible?

What Is The Best Final Expense Lead To Use?

The best final expense mailer is becoming harder for independent final expense agents to find. Discover the different variations in final expense direct mail leads to determine which final expense mailers is best to use. In this section, I will discuss the fundamentals of lead generation in final expense. Specifically, we will discuss how to find the best final expense mailer and what that mailer consists of.

I talk to a lot of agents and almost always we discuss is, "What final expense direct mail lead should I use?" I'm focusing my discussion on two of the most common final expense mailers available. I'll then give you my personal opinion on each type, based off of years selling final expense.

The first piece here is what I would call the "standard fare" 2015 Benefit Information final expense mailer.

The first line of the lead card reads, "You may qualify for a state-regulated life insurance program to pay for final expenses for just pennies a day." That line right there is what the WHOLE lead piece hinges upon. The fact that it says, "life insurance" and then it says, "it costs pennies a day."

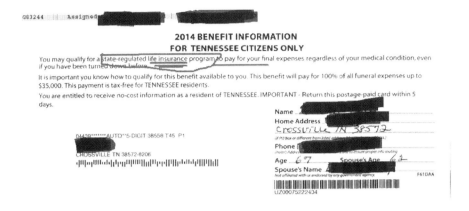

When you talk about final expense marketing and you talk about final expense mailers, **what this final expense mailer says dramatically affects the kind of quality of response that you get as well as the volume of response.**

Along with a general decline in response rates to non-internal marketing list, there is an inverse relationship between specificity of the direct mail lead piece and the aggregate response rate. **If you laser target into a group of prospects or names on a list, the more specific the wording of the final expense mailer piece, the less response you're going to get.**

For example, if you send a final expense mailer that says, "Hey, send this in if you want to buy life insurance. We'll send somebody over to talk to you about it unexpectedly to try to pressure you into a deal," you won't get very many people responding back. But if you get a final expense mailer that's more generic and less specific, you're going to get a lot of people replying that aren't necessarily as interested in buying.

The final expense mailer piece that says "life insurance" is what I would consider to be a very good balance of specificity and vagueness. What I mean by that is that first line there, the line that says, "life insurance that costs pennies a day," that tells the person responding that it is life insurance and that it's something that's going to cost something.

So what happens is the people who respond are kind of curious because the piece, itself, looks official. It may be government-related; they may get a deal off of it because of this. But they know they need life insurance. So the people sending this card back are a lot better quality respondents.

Next, you've got almost something that's exactly the same final expense mailer piece, except that it says, "You may qualify for a state-regulated program to pay for your final expenses, regardless of your medical condition." This one is what we call the 'vanilla version.' It hints at what the whole thing's about. But it never really nails it down with specificity.

2015 BENEFIT INFORMATION FOR
GEORGIA RESIDENTS

You may qualify for a state regulated program to pay for your final expenses regardless of your medical condition even if you have been turned down before.

It is important that you know how to qualify for this benefit available to you. This benefit will pay 100% of all funeral expenses up to $35,000.00. This program is tax free for Georgia residents.

You are entitled to receive free information as a resident of Georgia. Return this postage-paid card today.

***** SCH 5-DIGIT 30742

Fort Oglethorpe, GA 30742-3720

Signature

Age 65   Spouse's Age 67

Phone (   )

Not Affiliated With Any Government Agency   E-64

As I stated earlier, a final expense mailer like this with fewer specifics will give a higher response rate. This vanilla card will increase your response rate, probably, 25 to 50%, but the quality of response is typically decreases.

In my experience, you'll get more blank cards back or people who write down their name without their phone number. You have to make an added effort to door-knock these people. There are a lot more people that are requesting what I jokingly call "*Mutual of Obama*", or free life insurance. They sincerely are interested in some sort of state-specific regulated program to pay for their deadbeat ass.

The argument among more experienced agents is, "A lead is just an opportunity. It doesn't matter what the lead says. I'm just going to work whatever I get the most of and make the best out of it." If that works for you, great! Because all I care about is results. **And if the generic final expense mailer gives you better results, and allows you sell more policies, then go for it.**

In my experience with vanilla cards, I get results. I get people responding back. A lot of them know it's about life insurance. **But I'll get a lot more junk to filter through.**

However, I get more people who want free final expense burial life insurance. I get more people who don't put their contact information down and they're just a lot harder to reach. So, based on my approach to selling final expense life insurance, I just don't really care for the lead piece.

Whereas the final expense direct mail piece I used that says life insurance on it, I know that these people probably understand what the deal is about. They're not all geniuses that send the card in, don't get me wrong. But many know what to expect when they send in a card that says life insurance on it. So you'll get a better quality in your response.

The downside is that with a more specific final expense mailer, you will get a reduction in response. In my Final Expense Agent Mentorship Program, I have access to a fixed price final expense mailer program using the specific lead piece mentioned above at a guaranteed price point. You don't have to pay the higher prices that really are the norm in the final expense business now for a final expense mailer that says life insurance.

Why Modern-Day Final Expense Is Bought, Not Sold!

I was reading an article on a final expense life insurance think-tank type of organization's website, where the author was discussing the long-term projections of the intermingling of technology with the traditional approach of selling face-to-face in the final expense burial insurance business. In the process of describing the changes the final expense business is going through, the author mentioned a familiar phrase that most life insurance agents have heard: "**Life insurance must be sold, it is not bought**."

Regarding the final expense niche, I have to take the opposing side to that "old wives's tale" of a claim. Let me explain. In the final expense business, agents typically deal with people who are fifty and older, much more commonly older than sixty; all have had health problems, and most are on a fixed income. Our prospects are at an age where their friends have died, even their spouses have died, certainly their parents have died, and they all understand the pain and the cost of what it takes to bury somebody.

The type of person that responds to these cards *already is sold on why they should have life insurance,* or sold on why they should have some kind of policy to protect them. You don't have to persuade this type of person on why final expense life insurance is important – **they already get it!**

What you need to sell your prospect on is why YOUR life insurance is better than the alternative options. This subtle, differentiating factor makes a dramatic difference in how you use and run a final expense business in a couple of different ways. First of all, acknowledging that you are prospecting your leads for BUYERS who are already SOLD on burial insurance means that you realize that *final expense is a numbers game*.

Understand that this doesn't mean presenting, learning how to fact-find, and how to present things in language that elicits excitement and urgency is not important; what it means is this business is about finding the people that "GET" it and understand the reason and necessity for final expense life insurance. The other thing an agent realizes is that a successful final expense sales career is about identifying as quickly as possible *if a lead is a suspect or a prospect*.

A suspect is somebody who replies to a lead card and may have a marginal level of interest but DOES NOT fit the requirements and parameters of becoming somebody who's a PROSPECT, which is somebody who is highly likely to buy because they fit the prerequisites for someone who would fit what we have to sell.

It's our job as a sales person to identify if the lead that we're sitting in front of actually matches the requirements for us to actually do business with them, and a very skilled final expense salesman will pre-qualify upfront as quickly and as succinctly as possible whether or not this particular person actually matches the requirements of somebody who would likely buy.

Let me give you a real live example of this. I ran nine appointments and sold six applications. The very last appointment I ran was a final expense direct mail lead card. I sat down with a husband and a wife; they told me up-front that they're just kind of looking around to see what this is about, and didn't really any show interest. Those are what we call "knee-jerk reactions" - you still continue the presentation and not let that kind of initial reaction deter you.

I gave my presentation, asked for their business, and still had absolutely zero interest. At that point, I realized this person is a suspect, NOT a prospect. The husband didn't have any urgency to buy, despite me showing them something that would fit the budget range they said was comfortable. The husband had already experienced heart attacks, open heart surgery, stints, defibrillators-- all before the age of fifty! This guy is literally at death's door at fifty-one and he still doesn't get it.

If this guy is TRULY a prospect for final expense life insurance, he's going to do it now. If he doesn't get it by now, DESPITE his horrific health experiences, I can't fix stupid and will not spend time on a guy who doesn't understand the necessity for burial insurance because this guy, of ALL people, should get it!

Further, there's no way that I'm going to spend an hour with this dude to sell him on why he should have life insurance. If it doesn't fit his budget, if he is not open and engaged in the sales process, **I'm not wasting time on a loser that flat-out DOES NOT CARE.**

This is a prime example of what this business is about. You notice I did nine appointments. I sold six applications. I didn't put a gun to any of these people's heads to buy from me, and I guarantee you when I sat down with these people they knew it was about life insurance, they understood the necessity for life insurance, and once we found something that fit their budget and I sold them on the reasons why they needed to buy from ME, they bought. It was that simple!

And the last thing that this shift in perception brings with how to sell life insurance is that people not only need to be sold on what policy is BEST for THEM, but they need to be SOLD ON YOU as the expert in this burial insurance business.

The person that sells the insurance is THE primary factor of whether or not they're going to buy. People need to trust somebody with their life insurance decisions. If they don't like you, to some extent, they probably won't buy. But if they don't trust you, they sure as hell ain't buying from you. That is why when you sell insurance, you've got to make them trust you as the expert, as somebody who gets it and who will do the job, and provides the best solution for that particular customer -- that's what salesmanship is about.

I remember some sales guru said once is that sales about finding your man, find your guy -- the guy that "gets" it -- that's what the final expense burial insurance business is about. I urge you to keep these thoughts and wisdom in perspective and remember that when you're out there running a bunch of appointments with a bunch of deadbeats and thinking there's something wrong with you. More likely than not, if you know what you're doing in this business and you're running the appointments, it's the deadbeats, not you!

Why Agents Fail in the Final Expense Business

The reason agents fail at the final expense business is actually pretty simple. Let me throw a factor that holds true really in any sales endeavor.

Ninety percent of all salespeople flop out within the first year.

Now, why is that? The truth is it doesn't matter. It is not exclusive to final expense. It's true of ALL sales businesses.

Why is that the case?

First of all, **the reasons agents fail is because first of all the give up on themselves**. They go into the business with aspirations that didn't match reality. There are many skills to develop to successfully sell final expense that isn't readily obvious to the average person. Final expense sales training is something that takes months if not years to develop. Many people don't understand that sales are entirely different from corporate position. You have emotional ups and downs almost daily. Being on straight commission, you literally wake up every morning unemployed without any guaranteed income.

If you don't have experience, there is nothing to really prepare you for it until you understand what that is like and you are living it.

It is something that many people just can't handle.

Then the other reason people fail in this business is because they don't get involved with the right agency to help train them, to prepare them for the realities. They get involved with a business that sells "Blue Sky," meaning all the benefits of a lifestyle of Final Expense and none of the gritty work that it takes to succeed in the long-run.

Also, new final expense agents fail because they get involved in an agency that is designed to short change them and squeeze the dollars out of them at a ridiculous rate. It ends up being a revolving door type of sales agency.

It is important that agents do their research on the front-end. Talk to different agencies. Get a feel for your managers' personality type. Figure out who has been successful. How long agents have been working with them? Ask for proof. Are they transparent with what to expect as far as commission and percentage advancements based on merit and production history?

What do you get for your investment? Because the Manager makes money off of your production. You just have to make sure value is there. Take the time to ask these questions. Again, it is really important you are reading this because most agents don't go into this business even knowing what to ask, much less what to expect.

Many final expense agents don't understand that you must come into this business with a business mindset. Most agents buying direct mail and won't have the benefit of a referral network or an existing book of business. Instead, they have to buy leads to get going.

My recommendation is about $4,000 to $5,000 for a Direct Mail approach, or if you have less than that keep a full-time job and then also you know if you got $1,000 to $2,000 minimum for a telemarketing approach.

You got to start on the right foot. You got to be prepared for the ups and downs. You have to be willing to work through it with the understanding that the long-term is what makes it worth having. What makes it all worthwhile.

That's the reasons why most agents fail. The important thing is to go into this with the right group that shows you transparently what to do. When you know that you have got that on your side, it is really up to you.

Do you have the X-Factor to work hard and follow the system that is laid out upon you?

That's really the ultimate determinate of your success or failure.

How To Succeed In the Final Expense Business

How does a new final expense agent in training succeed in the final expense business?

An agent I respect highly who brought me into this business once said, *"Final expense is simple, but it is not easy."*

Final expense is simple because the products aren't complicated. Final expense sales are a one-call close 90% of the time. Final expense carriers pay a high commission payout. The lead generation process is duplicatable.

However, this business is anything but easy! You deal with all sorts of personalities and all sorts of environments. You have ups and downs. Most likely, all agents will at one point question themselves and the decision of working in the final expense industry due to having a rough time selling.

The weekly swings in success can really affect people who aren't of emotional discipline. How do you manage the head game and succeed in the final expense business? Here are the principles I teach agents to follow when entering the final expense business:

1) **Final expense sales agents that succeed have strong work ethic.** Whether the agent is captive or independent doesn't matter; they get out there and work and do whatever it takes to succeed. They

work 6 days a week, sometimes 10 to 12 hours a day in the field, not counting follow-up work and hours of paperwork. They try to work every single lead they get. They make every second count that they are in the field.

2) Final expense agents commit to direct mail every week.

The final expense is a business driven primarily by direct mail. As a rule of thumb, always copy what the top 10% of sales reps in any industry. And the top 10% of final expense agents work some sort of lead generation into their business model on a weekly basis.

3) **Be an independent agent.** What we see is the best agents in this business are independent. Meaning they are not tied down to one insurance carrier. They have the option to sell multiple carriers. This gives them more options and better final expense sales opportunities.

4) **Agents are properly capitalized**. Now, there are ways to work leads free or to find or generate your own leads for next to nothing. However, again with the desire with the understanding you need direct mail, or you need paid for lead generation and that is what most agents do.

Agents need to think about how they are capitalized when they come into this business. Many agents failed before they have the opportunity to succeed because they did not save enough to weather the inherent ups and downs.

It is suggested to save 3 to 6 months of money for expenses, or keep a full-time job and start Final Expense out on a part-time basis. Nothing is wrong with that. For final expense direct mail, you need between $4,000 and $5,000 in investable money to get started.

How Final Expense Like Most Activities Is All About How Hard You Work

I posted an article on LinkedIn entitled, "The Truth About Final Expense Commissions" I had a couple agents making some comments with one agent, in particular, saying something that disturbing.

This agent said, in so many words, that talented agents get bogged down by the realities of final expense-- the leads, commission levels, etc. That kind of struck a chord with me because on a larger note, one of the things you always hear about is whether salesmen are born or made. In other words, is there a difference between actual talent and work ethic? **I'm here to tell you that work ethic is crucial and the differentiating factor to success in learning how to sell final expense.**

I hate when I hear people really prop up the idea of talent or natural skill because a lot of times people who are very talented are also extremely lazy. The media loves to talk about sports professionals and other people who make it in life as "talented", but very commonly they fail to actually tell the entirety of the story, which is the hard work that was brought along to develop that person into a skilled professional, be it in sports or in sales or in any endeavor.

That's always very frustrating because I think of myself-- I think I'm a pretty smart individual, but I can tell you 15 years ago, even 5 or

10 years ago, I was extremely afraid to even pick up the phone and call Pizza Hut to order pizza. I just hated talking to strangers, I'm a natural introvert.

I was definitely NOT born a salesman, and so it took years of persistence, years of changing my mindset, especially when learning how to sell final expense. I've heard it for years. "You have got to push yourself out of the comfort zone." You have to basically risk failure to possibly get to the next level of what you're capable of.

In sales, when it comes to talent, it's so overrated because the guys that win in this business came with the willingness to take a risk and get out there to learn how to sell final expense, by knocking on doors, taking the risk of getting rejected. Taking the risk of getting yelled at and doors slammed in their face. Taking the risk of getting embarrassed, going on calls continuously and not making sales.

That is the risk and the hard work that's involved in any endeavor and definitely, when learning how to sell final expense. **So when I hear about people who talk about the greatness of talent, I think it's a bunch of crap.**

Want to know the secret on how to sell final expense successfully? Get your 20 to 25 leads each week, and make it your life's mission to take that stack of leads, hit the door Monday morning and knock every one of those doors. I promise you this. Even if you are an average sales person, if you get out there and you see the people and you do whatever it takes short of breaking in, you will sell more deals than the talented guy who's too good to work hard, or who thinks of himself too highly to actually get out there and work his butt off.

I felt obligated to do this post because it always frustrated me when people talk and over-exaggerate the importance of talent, especially when talking about how to sell final expense. Sure, it's important, but so is the work ethic. We don't hear enough of that and it's important to shine the light on, if you're looking into final expense, that hard work is the differentiating X-factor that makes all the difference in this business.

Remember that you don't have to be a great salesman. What you need is an open mind and you need to be willing to work 6 days a week for as long as possible to work every last single lead that you get every week and that's how you develop into a successful final expense agent.

The best final expense agent will EMBRACE being a replacement artist.

When a final expense agent gets called a "replacement artist," typically it is referenced as a slur. Most captive agencies trying to feed the Kool-aide to their sales force call us independent agents "replacement artists" in a negative fashion. They do this to brainwash them from going independent. These captive agencies don't want agents seeing that actively seeking to make replacements where appropriate is actually a good thing!

I had a comment pulled off of one of my YouTube videos called 'The Truth About the Final Expense Business.' It's my most popular YouTube videos for learning about the final expense industry. I think every final expense agent should invest time listening to the audio, as it gives important insight into how the final expense business REALLY works.

Unfortunately, captive agents like the one who commented on my YouTube video don't always agree. Before it was pulled, the comment said, "Replacement is such bullshit. Seventy-eight million baby boomers-- it's enough business out there for all companies. Only replacement artists and people with no place to go worry about replacement, it's not enough."

Seeing this post, the first thing I thought was, "This sounds like one of these captive final expense agent companies."

To my shegrin, in just two minutes of research, this crybaby commenter turns out to be a manager for one of the most notorious and well-known captive final expense companies. Needless to say, I wasn't surprised.

Why wasn't I surprised? First of all, **these captive final expense agent companies usually are "one trick ponies."** They present to Mildred and present a life insurance product notoriously known as the most overpriced product on the market amongst agents. They use sales gimmicks to convince the prospect their product is different to attain the sale.

As an experienced final expense agent, if you only have one product to sell, you will eventually not offer the best value product to your client. This begs the question. If a final expense agent replaces an overpriced product with a better-priced product, how could you rationally dispute her decision to better her life insurance situation?

The truth is the final expense agent that works at these captive carriers has to concoct some sales bull to pitch their garbage. And understandably they get upset.

That's why they call us replacement artists! Because they are upset, they are losing the sale.

There is a correct way to sell as a final expense agent. And while it does sucks to get replaced, every final expense agent gets replaced eventually. It's part of this business. The reason you MUST be a final expense agent replacement artist is - **There are many final expense carriers, and the product mix shifts every 3 to 6 months**.

Back in 2013, 5-Star Life Insurance was the "cat's meow" - it was a perfect final expense product. Then the Home Office tightened up tremendously on underwriting and raised prices. As a final expense agent, if you were pigeonholed into that one product, your business would have most definitely been adversely affected.

You do NOT want to be caught in the middle of your only carrier increasing pricing, tightening underwriting, or short-changing you on its new commission structure. If you only have a hammer to screw something into the wall, well, you're screwed, aren't you? This is why being an independent final expense agent, having access to multiple carriers is how you get the job done most efficiently and the most effectively.

In the final expense business, when somebody force-feeds an inferior product on a prospect, in the form of unnecessarily high pricing or poor value of coverage - don't be shocked when the "replacement artist" comes in and replaces your policy. There is always a final expense agent that will replace their own Grandma's coverage for something worse off, and so it can't be understated that everybody that replaces isn't necessarily ethical. **But that DOESN'T mean everybody selling for captive organizations is ethical, either.** Just because you're replacing doesn't mean you're a bad guy. If you go into it, though, and you do lead with the concept of wanting to get your client the best option for their bottom dollar, which is what the client will appreciate.

Why do they appreciate a final expense agent for replacing their coverage? Because we deal with are people on a fixed income. Most of our leads make as little as $700 to $800, and as much as $1,100 to $1,200 a month. If you can save them $10 to $15 a month, or $150 to $250 a year, OR if you can get your client $8,000 for the same price they got through the captive agent for $5,000 in coverage, I am doing something better than what the last guy did. There's nothing scandalous about that.

Everyone wants the best deal on what they are buying - life insurance, a printer, a computer, a house. If we have our own self-interest in mind, we prefer working with the company that will do that. That's why it's dangerous working for these captive companies as a final expense agent. You will be replaced when a half-decent agent comes behind you.

If Mildred has her car break down 6 months from now and that guy that walks in at the right time and she needs to save money, I guarantee you-- it doesn't matter how great of a final

expense agent you are, 9 out of 10 times the new guy is going to replace you, especially if you took advantage of a situation where you sold a rip-off product.

I'm glad to be a final expense agent that values being a replacement artist. If you're an independent agent, you should be too. It's all about doing the right job for the customer. It's all about getting them the best value and the best price.

And remember it's not always about price that causes replacement. Many times policies are replaced because giving immediate coverage where the captive company final expense agent could only provide a modified two-year waiting period policy. When you see an obvious opportunity to improve the client's situation, what are you supposed to do? Not give this person a better deal like the commenter said? Or at least show them the other side of the coin? This is why any final expense agent manager that suggests replacement is for fools KNOW their company's inherent weakness. What they are doing is trying to pass the blame versus figuring out a strategy to improve.

What Do You Wear On Final Expense Appointments?

I come from the kind of background where I always like to dress nice -- not suits kind of thing but, you know, business casual, which means slacks, button-down shirt and yeah-- a tie too. However, as I've gotten involved in this business of final expense, **I've realized all that stuff doesn't really matter as much as I thought it did.** So what do you wear when you're out in the field for final expense? How do you know what you wear is appropriate?

Well, you should try to dress one notch above your clientele; that doesn't mean you need to dress business executive. First, you've got to understand who your clientele is and if you've run enough final expense appointments, you know your clientele ain't exactly business executive. Usually, they're just in jeans and a t-shirt if you're lucky, while other times they are dressed in their *"See-Through-Moo-Moo."*

I started out wearing khakis, button-down shirts, polos. But four years into it I finally realized that I could wear jeans! On business calls! And I do fine. As far as my shirt goes, I wear a golf polo type shirt most of the time. It is embroidered with a carrier I work with because I like them and it kind of gives me a little bit of credibility. The value you give somebody in this business, as far as your prospects go, is dependent upon what you tell them and how you educate them on their options for final expense and so **my point is that dress means less in this business than in others.**

Now you do need to be put together. You shouldn't have your shirt hanging out, pants around your butt, you know. You should try to look decent, but you don't have to be Mr. Suave.

Dressing like this hasn't made a dent in the quality of sales and business I've conducted since I made the transition. So lighten up about the dress, guys. Just put on some clothes that look halfway decent, tuck your shirt in, and don't look like a fool. But hey, get out there and talk to people because that's what we really should be concerned about, is how are we going to see more people to sell more final expense life insurance to?

What to Carry into the House
When you're on a Final Expense Appointment

When running a final expense appointment, always bring the direct mail lead piece in. If you do not, it can cause some initial objections because half of these people won't recall sending the card in. However, if you shove something in their face and they signed their name, you'll have a better chance to get in the door without issue.

Showing a copy of the card the recipient sent in gives you a little bit more time to present and build a case. I plan ahead where I'm door-knocking based on my schedule. I don't carry all my final expense leads with me. I select the ones that are in the area that I'm going to be in.

I carry my appointment schedule with me as well as well as my applications in an accordion file. I buy the big ones one can get from Staples. They allow carrying lots of applications, brochures, rate guides, underwriting guides, etc. Make sure you keep GermX Hand Sanitizer on you at all times! I keep the industrial size handy in my car and always use it between appointments. Everything else I keep in the back of my car's trunk. I segment applications and brochures into their own separate cardboard box, so if I need to go back for additional supplies, I can hit the trunk and take everything I need.

How To Door Knock
Final Expense Leads

Final expense lead prospecting occurs in one of two forms. First, the agent phones the lead for a face-to-face appointment. Second, the agent shows up unannounced, otherwise known as a "door knock." In this section, we will cover how to effectively door knock direct mail leads so you can realize more appointments and more sales opportunities.

Physically showing up unannounced and door-knocking a final expense lead is the most efficient way for a new agent to maximize the value of his lead, which we will cover in-depth in a short moment.

How to Initiate a Door Knock: First, park your car in the lead's driveway. Leave the car running and the door open. This gives the appearance that you are only briefly stopping by, which lowers the initial reaction not answer the door. Once at the door, knock 7 to 10 times firmly. Do not beat down the door like a cop would. But don't knock weakly. Next, take a step or two back from the door and fix your eyes on the peephole, watching for the light in the door to turn dark. When the light from the peephole turns dark, there is someone looking out at you, so make sure you wave at them to give them more reason to answer the door.

When they answer the door, go right into your introduction script outlined below:

"Hey, Mrs. Jones. My name is David Duford, and I am here about this card that you sent in (*show it to her*) a few weeks ago. Most people send this card in because they are looking for some kind of information on taking care of their final expenses like burial and cremation.

"I'm the guy that delivers the information you requested, and I was between appointments and wanted to see if you had 5 minutes for me to show you how this works."

At the door, your prospect will do one of two things: she will let you in immediately, or begin quizzing you at the door.

If you get statements like, **"I am really busy," simply tell them, "I drove here from an hour away; I promise to give the short version and will be done in 10 minutes; is that OK?"**

If they still resist or are insistent they don't have time at that moment, **the next step is to set an appointment for the same day or the following day.**

To succeed at door-knocking your final expense leads, you have to communicate effectively through proper use of body language. For example, when the prospect opens the door, make immediate eye contact, widen your eyes, and smile big. Stand tall, come off with a friendly disposition and be easy-going and relaxed. Speak positively with energy! There are several reasons why all new final expense life insurance agents should door-knock all their leads.

The first reason is that more people now than ever heavily screen their phone calls. If the person does not recognize the number, they do not pick up. Many great sales opportunities are lost for agents who only set appointments, as many leads would easily buy final expense life insurance if the agent would just simply show up at the lead's door.

The second reason is that phoning for appointments is a unique skill set that takes time to develop. Many agents will lose out on sales opportunities because they fumble on the phone and come off as goofballs to the prospect. However, we all are used to speaking with people face-to-face, and it is easier for the agent to come off genuinely face-to-face versus using the phone, and usually leads are more forgiving in person and less likely to turn you down.

Using Sticky Notes To Optimize Your Success Door Knocking Your Leads

What happens after you knock on the door... and no one answers? How does door knocking final expense leads successfully work if you can't get in the door?

It's called "sticky notes!"

Most final expense direct mail leads reference sending the reply card back if they want additional information. Our job as final expense salespeople is to "deliver" the information. How we do so is NOT specified, meaning we can show up in-person to deliver the information to the respondent.

How do delivery slips come into play when door knocking for final expense? These sticky note slips look like slips your friendly neighborhood FedEx or UPS carrier uses to notify you about a package you weren't home to receive. You can list your name, your number, the person you're trying to reach on the note. Moreover, the sticky note creates an important level of urgency, saying, "Please call back within the next 24 hours."

As you may understand, many of our leads incorrectly think that this is some kind of package. And that's why we use them to take advantage of that presupposition.

The majority who are left the notes call back. And when they do, you know they're home. Meaning you know where to go next in your prospecting efforts. Hopefully, you can see how this is a very powerful sales presentation tactic to use. Using sticky notes when door knocking for final expense sales allows you to optimize your time. And if you love to door knock, these sticky notes will measurably improve your set appointment ratio.

What's the downside to using sticky notes for final expense door knocking? First, a lot of these people will continue to call if you didn't show, even into the earliest morning hours. I've had leads call 4 or 5 times after 10 o'clock at night until 8 o'clock in the morning. It's ridiculous but does happen from time to time.

What I recommend is to set up kind of Google Voice number for your sticky note calls to forward. That way you protect your private cell phone number, but also, get email notifications letting you know someone has tried to call. The other downside is that you really need to make sure in your state that these notes are legal to use. I know of an agent that was fined due to these sticky notes. In the Department of Insurance's mind, it was labeled as "deceptive advertising."

Use your own legal counsel before you make the decision to use these notes. I've used them in the Southeastern states without any problems. I've heard of people using them fine in some mid-western states. The good thing is they work well when you go final expense door knocking. It's a great way for a guy who is busy in the field to stay very focused and tight and always be talking to people that actually are home. The sticky notes give you a little bit more help in that regard to let you get in the door when you can.

How To Sell Burial Insurance
When The Lead Won't Answer The Door!

In this section, I am covering how to sell burial insurance when your good-for-nothing burial insurance lead decides to no-show you. Having personally experienced the same issues learning how to sell burial insurance, these tactics work very well and come highly recommended. The bottom line is to stay efficient. You've got to quickly flush out bad leads from the good ones.

Scenario #1. You knock on the final expense appointment's door and see a car in the driveway. However, no one answers. Do you get pissed and think this lead is trying to avoid you? Not necessarily! A lot of these leads just can't hear too well.

My first recommendation is to pound the door down. If that doesn't work, I use my phone and I call them. Don't feel any reservations calling. Many times they'll hear the phone better than a door knock. This gives you another shot to sell them burial insurance

Also, make sure **to knock the side door instead of the front door**. Most people don't use their front door with any regularity. Always try different doors like side doors and back doors. I would probably try knocking all available doors first before calling.

Scenario #2: You've knocked all the doors. You've even tried calling. And you are getting nowhere. How do you sell burial insurance to this guy?

Here's an effective trick to solicit the lead to pick up the phone. When you call, most likely you'll get a voicemail. Most people never pick the phone up on a call that they don't recognize. **Assuming they don't pick up, hang up the phone without leaving a voicemail, wait about 5-10 seconds, and then call again.**

You'll be shocked at how many people will pick up on the second attempt. The psychology behind this working is that when they see the same number call them back immediately, they figure the call must be important, and are more likely to pick up. I started doing this in my personal production and this made a significant business in getting people to pick up the phone.

Scenario #3: What happens if they still don't pick the phone up? I stumbled upon this idea because I got tired of driving two, three, even four hours away to an appointment, just to get stood up. I've gotten to the point where I hate wasting time on idiots that aren't respectful of mine.

So what's the technique? **Leave a marginally-angry voice mail.**

The key to making the voicemail technique work is in your tonality. You definitely do not want to sound like a jerk. But you don't want to sound easy-going about no-showing you either. You want to sound a slight bit irritated but communicate in an authoritative way that they screwed up your schedule and they need to call you as soon as possible. Nothing gets a no-shows attention than coming off like this! You want them feeling guilty because they wasted your time, and that they broke their promise.

Here's what I say when I leave the voicemail:

"Hey, this is David. I'm here for our appointment at 10 o'clock that we had set over the weekend, and you're not here. (slight pause) I actually drove all the way from Chattanooga to Gainesville to see you, it's a 2 ½ hour drive, and you promised Michelle that you'd be here, and it's put me behind big time in my schedule and so I'm hoping you're stuck somewhere or something came up but I need you to call me back today at 423-432-4323 when you get this message right away. I'm pretty busy the rest of the day, my schedule is really jam-packed. I may be able to see you, but you need to call me right away when you get this message so I know what's going on. Again, the number's 423-432-4323."

You'll be shocked that around half of these people will call me back and they'll tell me that, "I tried calling, I just wasn't interested, blah, blah, blah," you get the same kind of reception as you would at the door if you finally caught them, or you'll get people who are really apologetic that are interested that just totally forgot.

An added benefit of these terse-sounding voice mails is they do a great job of qualifying whether or not the lead is serious. Combined with the sticky notes, I get about half of them to call me back. If they can call me back and have expressed their apologies for no-showing me in combination with sharing some interest in what I am selling, they're the kind of person I want to spend time to get back in front of. On the flip side, if the lead never takes the time to call back, they're the jerk-offs I don't want to deal with! I'm not going to fight to get in front of these no-shows jerks.

Three Reasons To Door
Knock Final Expense Leads

Door-knocking final expense leads is an important skill to develop. It's one of the easier ways to prospect final expense leads, and is important to master in a career that has a lot of nuances, technical issues, and so forth that need to be mastered. I believe door knocking is one of the best ways for new final expense agents to effectively prospect their leads.

Why should new agents door knock final expense agents? As a new agent, you have to accept the fact that you don't know what you don't know. There's a lot in this business that you'll learn simply by trial and error, and an important factor to consider is that you're going to have to door knock final leads to maximize the results out of your leads. If you only set appointments over the phone, you're going to miss out on sales opportunities because you don't know how to effectively set appointments. That's a separate skill set that takes time to develop, but does not allow the best results from the beginning if you're brand new to phoning for appointments.

Door-knocking final expense leads is the best way to get the most out of each batch of leads that you purchase. Why? It's not nearly as difficult for a prospect to slam the door in your face as it is to hang up on you. You're probably going to have a much higher chance to talk to the person that sent the card in face-to-face. This allows for more follow-through; you'll get more opportunities to ask what their existing coverage is, what their thoughts on it are, and possibly see if there's any opportunity to replace coverage. More leads now than ever are not answering the phone unfamiliar phone calls. People screen calls more heavily with the advent of caller ID, which is why old fashioned door knocking can be used to overcome this trend towards call screening.

Door knocking final expense leads is simple. It's very easy to door knock final expense leads effectively, and there are only a few core basics. The main thing is making sure that you make eye contact. Also, make sure you're dressed appropriately, always offer a handshake and just be yourself! It's so much easier to do that than to use the phone, because the phone removes body language out of the conversation which accounts for the majority of the effectiveness of our communication skills.

I'm not one that feels like you've got to do the "two-step shuffle," or you have to lean yourself in and start walking in the door. If you simply introduce yourself, tell them why you're there, and that you need a few minutes to talk about what it is they requested, that's all that's necessary. Door knocking final expense leads is the best way to prospect as a beginner. Given enough time, you do want to develop the skill to set appointments over the phone, to maximize efficiency, but even to that point, there are still final expense agents that have been doing this business for years that still door knock because they get much better follow-through with a batch of leads doing that versus utilizing the phone.

Should I Hire A Final
Expense Appointment-Setter?

Many new agents are not comfortable making phone calls to final expense leads to set appointments. I know I certainly didn't when I started my final expense career. Heck, I was afraid to pick up the phone and call the pizza man when I was a kid! When it comes to final expense sales and when it comes to setting appointments off of your final expense leads, there's really two different fields of thought.

The first field of thought is that **nobody works your final expense leads better than you do,** so it's your obligation to work those leads yourself and set appointments to maximize the return on your investment.

The second field of thought, which I'm more in that camp, there's a point of diminishing returns in that **if you do a lot of volume of leads, you really need to consider outsourcing the final expense appointment-setting activity** to somebody else in order to run more appointments.

Let me explain to you why I feel that outsourcing final expense appointment setting activity is a superior approach to selling final expense burial insurance. If you're buying fifteen to twenty leads a week, the activity level is not high enough that I would even look or bother with outsourcing your lead appointment-setting, unless you just have some morbid fear of doing the dials yourself. That's really the only circumstance where I would see that making sense.

Most final expense agents get involved in this business set their own appointments. It's an efficient way to get the most return on their investment. But if you're an agent that wants to do more than just the basic twenty-five leads a week, and you want to scale up and produce a lot of volume, you'll get to the point of considering hiring an appointment setter to set appointments. Certainly nobody will do a better job with your final expense leads than you. You paid for these leads, you own them, you're going to do better than hiring somebody else.

However, the bottom line is that your net after expenses will increase when you increase your leads and your activity in the field. Our job as a final expense sales person and as a business owner is to identify the activities and the core competencies that make us the most money. For a final expense sales person, the core competencies that make us the most money are our ability to get in front of a prospect to sell them and setting appointments to make that happen. And when you get to the point where you bridge that gap is when a final expense appointment-setter makes the most sense.

I outsource appointment setting to an appointment-setter. When I'm running direct mail leads, I'll run thirty to forty appointments a week, because I know I have a better ability to sell more final expense life insurance when I have pre-set appointments, versus going out there and door-knocking. I do better with appointments. I net more, and even if I'm not getting in front a higher ratio of the leads as I would door knocking, the ones I do get in front of have pretty good odds of being high-quality appointments.

For you final expense agents that are looking at an appointment setter and thinking, "Well, I either have," you know, "a fear of appointment-setting," or, "I have a lot of leads," or, "I want to take my business to the next level," an appointment-setter makes great sense, and I would highly recommend looking partnering with one as it will step your production volume considerably.

How To Set Final Expense Appointments By Phone

In this section, we are going to talk about how to set appointments using the phone. The goal is to show you how to use the phone to set appointments in an efficient manner.

Best Time to Call. The best time to call is anytime between 9 a.m. and 9 p.m.! Truly, any time of the day is a good time to call.

The most effective times of the days are first thing in the morning from about 9 a.m. to 11 a.m., or from about 4 to 5 o'clock until about 8:30 at night. Dinner time is always the best time to call. You will get more people picking up the phone since more people are home from their daily activities. You will find it is a better use of your time.

If you call on weekends, Saturday from 9 am to 12 pm works wonderfully. Sunday is even a great day if you are really motivated; 4 pm to 9 pm works great as people are getting back from church, and never anticipate a solicitor calling on a Sunday. Believe it or not, very few people actually complain about you calling on them for an appointment.

Appointment Setting Script. What do you actually say when you are on the phone with a lead? First of all, the goal is simply to set the appointment. Do not qualify the prospect. Do not go into the sales pitch. Your goal is to simply set an appointment to explain everything the lead is curious about.

The best-qualified lead is a lead agreeing to let you, a stranger, inside of her house for 10 minutes to discuss something they may possibly buy. This means that this lead most likely has a marginal level of interest in what we are selling, which is the best and only way to qualify someone over the phone. When phoning for appointments, you must be deliberate with the words you say. You must speak clearly, coherently, and loudly enough for the lead to both follow you and understand what you are saying. Generally speaking, slowing down your rate of speech to about 75% of your normal speed, and emphasizing the main words in the script will help you a bunch.

How does the script sound put together? When Mildred says hello, you say:

"Hey Mildred, this is Billy Bob calling about the information you requested. You **sent a card in** requesting information on our final expense programs. **I am calling you today because I will be in your area tomorrow and I want to set a 10-minute appointment to deliver the information** you **requested. Does 10 o'clock on Tuesday or 12 o'clock sound good?"**

Remember do not go into any more detail. You tell them who you are, why you are calling, and ask for the appointment. Hopefully, they will just set the appointment. But the reality is that there are always objections you have must handle.

The most common objections you are going to hear are, "What's this about," or, "I am busy," or, "I am not interested." How do you answer these types of objections? Very simply; just say enthusiastically, **"Hey that is fine and that is exactly why we need to meet. All I need 10 minutes to show you this information and what you do with it is up to you. How is tomorrow at 2?"**

This turn-around rebuttal works great with most objections you hear, with small variances depending on who you're talking to. For example, let's say the lead says, "I've got enough insurance.' Here's what you say to that:

"Hey, Mr. Jones I'm glad to hear that and the truth is everybody I meet with already has Life Insurance. This is about something totally different and all I need is 5 minutes to show you what it is about. How does tomorrow at 2 sound?

The reason this works is that (a) you acknowledge what the person said, and (b) you spark their curiosity while promising to be brief. Remember, they sent back the card for some reason, and most likely expected someone to follow-up with them, so you have to persist.

Final Expense Sales Training Section 1: Introduction and Rapport Building

Now that we've covered the prospecting section let's go into detail where the magic really happens: **the presentation**. Once you're inside the house, our focus shifts to overcoming initial resistance, building rapport, fact-finding, prequalifying the prospect, presenting the solution, and finally, only if it makes sense, you ask for the prospect's business. To clarify, the way I teach the final expense sales presentation process assumes a face-to-face appointment. Most of the sales process and verbiage is transferable to phone-based sales, but there are certain nuances unique to phone sales that I will not cover.

Details matter in sales. And how you pay attention to your attire makes a difference. Make sure that you are well-dressed when you give your presentations. "Well-dressed" means different things to different people. I recommend wearing business casual; properly-ironed khaki pants and a dress shirt or polo, and shined shoes is a simple and professional look for the people we do business with.

Please make sure you are clean-cut. That means you have shaved your face. Don't walk into a prospect's house looking like you just rolled out of bed. Make sure your breath doesn't smell like this morning's breakfast. Imagine someone walking into your own home looking scruffy and unkempt; are you going to do business with that person? Probably not. So please take the extra few minutes every day to pay attention to your personal presentation, because people do judge you by your appearance.

Four Parts To An Effective Final Expense Presentation

To successfully present final expense insurance to your prospects, you need to understand the four parts to an effective presentation:

1. **Build Trust**: Building trust consists of rapport-building, your 30-second commercial, and the ability to express your competence.

2. **Fact-Finding**: Fact-finding consists of asking the "Reason Why" question, the "3 Reasons" Question, and several "Deep Questions" in order for the prospect to establish the reason why you're present.

3. **Pre-Qualification**: This is how you determine whether or not you <u>can</u> and <u>want</u> to do business with your prospect.

4. **Presentation**: This is where we position ourselves against the competition, get feedback and engagement from the prospect, trial close on the concept, and end by asking for the business.

Understand this: **final expense is a <u>one-call close</u> presentation**. The four-part Presentation is not meant to be broken up over several calls. You have the capability to do all of this on the spot, even for you folks who have never sold anything. What you're about to learn is a low-pressure, honest, and straightforward sales presentation that will lead your prospect logically to buy from you for his own best interests in mind, while providing the emotional urgency to do it today.

What I will show you below is the exact sales presentation process I use every day in the field. My approach is always low-key. I don't high pressure close ever and always work for a mutually-beneficial sales proposition on a win-win basis. Remember, your solitary goal is to get in the door and close them. You cannot break this process up into two meetings. Your income will be half of what it could be, you will waste more time chasing "China eggs" and the final expense business will eternally frustrate you.

Part One – Building Trust

Building trust is vital to your success as a final expense agent. I define "building trust" as the combination of verbal and non-verbal communication that conveys both your understanding of the prospect and your expertise as a final expense agent. Broken down, building trust consist of how you build rapport with your prospect and how you communicate your expertise as an agent. Building trust is a process confined to the beginning of the sales process. It's built and reinforced throughout the sales process. However, you do take several steps in the very beginning of your presentation to build the foundation for trust.

Rapport-Building: Rapport is the idea of a well-understood, well-communicated relationship between one person and another. In sales, it's the edge a salesman gain when you take time to learn about the prospect. The importance of rapport is disputed amongst top salespeople, but the vast majority of salesman won't hurt their chances to win business if they connect with their prospects on more than a transactional level. This is especially the case in this market; the people you're dealing are older and appreciate personal relationships. Many of your prospects are lonely and isolated. Simply by listening for a few minutes to the lead's day will build a foundation level of rapport.

Here's how you build rapport. After you introduce yourself, pick out things that you see on the wall or on the table and ask questions about it. Trust me; this will be very easy to do. You will deal daily with grandparents, so you'll see their grandkids plastered all over their walls. Comment on the weather. Ask what they did before retiring and how retirement is treating them. Any kind of icebreaking attempt will usually be received well. Now, they may not go ahead and gush openly to you quite yet, but if you can, at least, get a conversation started, you'll begin to work away their initial sales resistance.

When I begin the rapport process, I make sure I'm smiling, jovial, and relaxed. I'll comment on the weather or the news, because these people have interest in the same thing and will respond back in kind. Eventually after doing the rapport process over several presentations, it becomes intuitive. You'll notice some will engage more in rapport-building, while others don't. You'll be able to feel out quickly whether or not a person responds well to rapport-building and adjust your approach accordingly.

Building Trust. Building trust is the single most important process in your entire sales presentation. Prospects only willingly hand over their money and banking account information to agents they trust; scumbags definitely won't get that information, and neither will nice clueless guys. Every prospect has un-materialized objections you must overcome. All prospects wonder, "Is this guy legitimate? Is he licensed? Who does he work for? What kind of person is this guy?" These are all objections you must overcome ahead of time to effectively assuage that concern.

Here's how I do it. After I sense we're ready to move on from rapport-building, I move into my **30-Second Commercial**. The 30-Second Commercial allows me to build legitimacy and establish professional and personal credibility, allowing me to further cement the all-important need for trust.

I start the 30-Second Commercial by saying, "Let me tell you a little bit about myself and what I do." First of all, if you are wearing a badge around your neck, hand it over so they can see and touch it. If you don't have a badge, use a laminated copy of your insurance license. The reason you hand the prospect your badge is the more senses you engage – sight, smell, feeling, hearing –you will internalize a greater sense of legitimacy in the prospect.

As I hand the badge over, I say, "My name is David Duford. I'm a licensed life insurance agent in the State of Tennessee, am responsible for mailing you that card you filled out and sent back. It's my job to follow up on people in Bradley County who send back these cards."

Next, if I haven't already, I hand them the laminated state life insurance license. Then I say, "I'm a licensed agent in the state of Tennessee. I've been in business for three years." Then you go on to tell them what other areas you work, and how many clients you have. Don't worry if you're brand new; tell them, "I've jumped through all the hoops, taken all the tests, well enough to satisfy the State of Tennessee's requirements to be a licensed life insurance agent."

The next step after establishing professional credibility is establishing personal credibility. This simple step cannot be underestimated. The more you humanize yourself and successfully draw yourself away from the typical salesperson model people have in their mind, the more business you will close.

Here's what I mean by "humanizing" yourself: your prospects are grandmothers, grandfathers, if not great-grandfathers and great-grandmothers. At the minimum, they have kids. And, if you are a parent, you enjoy children. We love them, we raise them, and you always enjoy seeing young life. To humanize myself, after I pack up my license and badge, I always say, "Life insurance is about the people you love and taking care of them so they don't have to take care of your burden. And that's why I always like to share pictures of my family." So I take out a picture of my son, my twins, and my wife, and hand it to my prospect.

The act of seeing my family always makes my prospect relax a little bit. The prospect realizes I'm a father that I'm out here working for the livelihood of my children and my wife. I'm not just some every other Joe average salesperson without any type of humanity.

I feel extremely convicted in showing a picture of family to humanize yourself. If you don't have family, if you don't have children, just you and your wife, if you're a former officer of the military, you can show them that you've served. Or if you have a dog, share a picture of Rover with your prospect.

Doing this simple act will positively affect people wanting to do business with you. Connecting beyond the idea of just a typical salesperson interaction, that's when people will go ahead and give you business. Because not only will you add value to their situation, but they'll realize, "This guy's a pretty nice guy, he knows what he's talking about, and I don't see anything wrong with him."

In summary, building rapport and trust is like building the foundation to your house; you cannot successfully sell final expense without it, and you must reinforce both trust and rapport as you continue through the presentation. Take as much time to build rapport and trust, because what do you have to lose? The truth is you need to have the odds stacked in your favor. I've talked to people for an hour before actually talking about life insurance. That's an exception to the rule; typically the process takes around 15 minutes max.

Why Trust Is More Important Than Rapport When Selling Final Expense Burial Insurance

One question I hear commonly from new salespeople is this: how much rapport is enough before actually focusing on selling final expense to the prospect? First, let's define rapport for those not familiar in sales: rapport is simply the act of creating conversation to get the prospect to like you. A very simple process, but can be a complicating endeavor. If you start to think of this stuff a little more than normal, you realize how much rapport should I say? What should I ask about? What shouldn't I? When should I stop it?

What kind of rapport should a brand new agent focus on? Newer agents should focus on building a level of rapport enough to get the prospect at ease with you. It may take 5 minutes. It may take an hour. I don't care, nor should you. If that's what it takes to get these people to lighten up, feel comfortable with the process and actually want to buy from you, then do what's necessary.

As a new agent selling final expense burial insurance, focus on asking basic, friendly, "ice-breaking" questions. Walk in, look at what they have, shake their hand, make eye contact with a little small talk. Maybe ask them about a picture, their golf clubs, the fish on the wall. A lot of these people are lonely. They don't get a lot of visitors. And many literally can't wait to spill their guts.

The idea is just to be genuine. Just be yourself! Don't feel like you have to have some 5-point rapport script. Just go in, be yourself, and be friendly. For experienced agents selling final expense burial insurance, where does trust-building come in? For advanced agents like myself, **rapport takes a back seat to trust-building.** What I'm most concerned about is making sure I exhibit myself as the "go-to" guy who knows his stuff about selling final expense burial insurance.

While I may not be the nicest guy they come across, I DO know how to get things done in a manner that's going to suit the client's needs and wants.

How does this affect rapport when I sell final expense? I don't focus on rapport nearly as much when I first started. I may come in, do a little bit of small talk, but I normally get right to the point. I get right down to business.

It's a little challenging to explain how selling final expense burial insurance at a more advanced level really is. When you've been doing this long enough, you've written more than a thousand policies, seen thousands of people, run every kind of presentation, you know what you're doing. And your prospects will naturally tell you are a "minsch" at selling final expense burial insurance!

You don't have to play Mr. Nice Guy to get to the point of why you're there. Nevertheless, some guys are great with the 'aw-shucks', nice-guy routine at selling final expense burial insurance. That's what does it for them. We all kind of have our shtick. But my goal for my agents is to develop themselves into confident final expense professionals who exude authority. The best agents simply demonstrate their skill by their natural disposition, body language, word choice, and conversation pacing.

You'll eventually grow to realize that selling final expense is truly all about trust. Moreover, selling final expense is about creating the environment for trust. Nevertheless, you want to do a little rapport-building. I still do it. Every agent does it to an extent. Selling final expense is not a wham-bam-thank-you-ma'am type of sale without any sort of connection.

Dealing With Knee-Jerk Objections

Have you ever walked into a sales presentation the lead says, *"Listen, I'm not buying anything, alright? I'm not buying, I just wanted the information. I'm just here to hear what you say. That's all I want."*

Most of you should be nodding, "Yeah, absolutely!"

The purpose of this section is to learn how to address knee-jerk objections, and how to subtly rebuttal them in the beginnings of your final expense sales presentation. I have been exchanging emails with a brand new agent regarding knee-jerk objections. He was in a final expense sales presentation where the lead replied to a direct mail final expense piece. The agent told me upon sitting at the dinner table, the lead said, "Listen, I'm not here to buy anything. I just want to hear what you've got to say, OK?"

Not knowing any better, the new final expense agent took his rebuttal seriously. The agent said, "That's totally fine. Let's just talk about the information." And so he did. The agent ONLY gave the information. He didn't give a full final expense sales presentation. Instead, he took that objection at face value.

Let's discuss why you should never do that.

Consider this: at the very beginning of your final expense sales presentation, how can a lead say they don't want to buy what you're selling, *when they don't know truly understand you're selling*? They THINK they know. But as a sales professional, you're the one giving them the information, right? And any buying decision can only be made AFTER you give that information, right?

Understand that any knee-jerk objection you hear in the beginning of your final expense sales presentation are almost universally made from ignorance. I'm not insulting the prospect. But they truly do not have any basis to make such a statement. It's important to understand that what you're telling them in your final expense sales presentation may be different than the perspective they have already pre-assumed before you arrived and sat down.

How do you get around this? And how do you know if that objection is legitimate or not? Here's how I look at it: you have to treat knee-jerk objections as a unfounded statement a lead uses, who's worried about making a bad buying decision.

Throwing out a baseless knee-jerk objection early on in your final expense sales presentation is a form of stress relief for your lead. It's how they deal with the stress of an impending sales situation. In a way, it's almost therapeutic for the lead, as it lowers his stress level. In your final expense sales presentation, to move around a knee-jerk objection, just acknowledge it and move on. You don't give it any more credence than just saying, "OK, that's fine." That's it. You don't say, "Well, OK, jeez-- what kind of information do you want?!"

Otherwise, you're handing control over to the lead. And control is everything in a final expense sales presentation. You want to THINK they have control, but yielding to a knee-jerk objection transfers control to the lead. Here's how the objection and rebuttal are scripted, "Listen, I know you're here about this card. I just want the information; I'm not interested in buying. I'm broke," just acknowledge it.

Say, "That's fine. I'm here to deliver the information," and then go on with your sales call, "What was the reason you sent the card in?" Don't spend any more time on it than that. This next point is critical.

You've got to continue the final expense sales presentation as if nothing was ever objected to. Understand that the perspective of a final expense lead in the beginning of the sales process is totally different than closer to the end. Once they begin to know who you are and begin to trust your authority on the subject matter, your leads will take your recommendation more seriously, and forget even objecting to your final expense sales presentation in the first place.

Is there any way to avoid rejection in final expense sales?

If you ever have sold anything, you know that rejection is just a normal part of the selling process. My goal of this section is to rationalize the concept of rejection for agents new to final expense sales. Many who are new to the final expense business may exhibit worry about what to expect from the sales process, so learning how to prepare yourself to handle rejection is extremely important.

First of all, let's face it: **rejection sucks.** Every final expense sales person gets rejection. Where they think a sale may have been, they lose it and they don't understand why. The final expense sales agent may feel personally slighted. Trust me; it's something we all deal with.

There's no salesperson out there that is immune from rejection. However, the final expense sales agents that succeed get over the pain of rejection faster and know how to deal with it. Here's the trick when it comes to rejection: rejection is not about YOU. **It's about rejecting your offer.**

Let's think about this. How can somebody reject you as a final expense sales person when they've only spoken to you for a couple minutes? They don't know you, how could they even reject you? What basis do they have to make a claim like that? If they do, they're an idiot!

If the lead doesn't buy what you're selling them, they're rejecting the product. They're rejecting the fact that they don't like what it is that you're offering. You have to understand a final expense sales call, you have to be totally confident in what it is that you're selling. They're not telling you, "You suck!" and that they don't like you.

You have to think about rejection and separate that from you. Because nobody can be rejected in a genuine fashion if they don't know you. They key here is that when you look at it that way, you don't take it personally. You should take it as a blessing! Because if they bought the product, and they did so on terms that didn't make sense for them, they're going to turn around and wake up the next day and cancel it anyway.

The crucial element of rejection is:

#1) Understand they're rejecting the product and they're just not right for the product.

Nobody is a prospect for everything, nobody sells everybody so get over it. People are going to say no, but they're saying no to your product, and not to you.

#2: It's important to have short-term amnesia.

This is something I do very well. I can have a horrible day where nobody buys anything I'm selling. The people are rude. The people are idiots! And I go home, I'm pissed off, but you know what? The next morning I've slept it off. I wake up enthused because it's a whole new day with totally different people. A whole new day with totally different leads, and I'm ready for action because I know, for as long as I've been in this business, that your fortunes can change within a day's worth of activity.

That's how I deal with rejection as a final expense sales agent. I've been rejected way more times than most sales people have, but in the same breath, I've been way more successful than most final expense sales people because I've been able to manage that rejection and compartmentalize it. I know they're just saying NO to my product.

Which leads me to my last point. Final expense sales agents that get hung up on rejection are either brand new agents to the final expense business, or are sales people that don't have enough people to talk to.

A great agent that once said, "All sales woes are because of a lack of prospects," and it's so true. Every rejection, every rebuttal, every problem in the process of selling final expense is amplified when I don't have anybody to talk to.

When I'm resting my hopes and dreams of financial final expense success on one or two appointments for that week, they're going to matter that much more than they should. My mentality in being involved in them is going to be that much more wrapped up than they would if I had 20 or 30 appointments.

You want to care, but not t-h-a-t much! And the way you get there is to have a large and consistent number of appointments each week. When you do you, you'll think, "I've got 14 other dudes to go to- - I'm going to sell some of them, so who cares what you think?"

You've got to make sure that you have leads coming in because that's what makes the difference between success and failure in this business. If you're resting it upon a few of these people, they're going to disappoint you. Your feelings are going to be hurt that much more because your ability to succeed or fail rests upon the tip of a pinhead. See the people, have people to see and don't think too much about the rejection because it's not about you, it's about the product.

Final Expense Sales Training Part 2: How To Fact-Find and Pre-Qualify

Many final expense sales agents ask me what part of the final expense presentation is the most critical to their success at closing new business.

Without any doubt, an agent must be able to effectively fact-find and pre-qualify as it is the most important skill to develop when selling final expense burial insurance.

Why is fact-finding and pre-qualifying critical to your success as a final expense agent? **Because effective fact-finding and pre-qualifying literally gives the agent the ammo necessary to make the sale, and quickly and early-on establishes whether the person they are meeting with is a prospect (someone pre-qualified to buy final expense life insurance) or a suspect (someone who may have interest, but lacks in a critical component that makes the suspect incapable of buying today).**

Effective fact-finding and pre-qualifying not only allows you to sell better, but it also allows you to determine what objections the client may have early on in the sales call, thus allowing the skilled salesperson the ability to address those issues early on.

How to Fact-Find for Final Expense

The next phase that we move into is the Fact-Finding phase. This is the phase we transition out from the Trust-Building Stage and into determining why the prospect sent our card back in, and to determine what needs and wants are motivating him. This step is vital, as fact-finding allows us to learn the logical and emotional motivations the prospect has for our product, as well as the level of commitment the prospect has in making solving the problem the prospect has.

As an aside, Fact-Finding and Building Trust phases are interchangeable. You can do one phase before the other. You might jump into the fact-finding stage initially due to a prospect unreceptive to rapport-building, then come back to it after you've established some of the facts up front.

Here's how I transition to the fact-finding phase:

"Mr. Prospect, do you know why I'm here today? I'm here because I received this green card from you in the mail (hand them the card). We sent that card to you a few weeks ago and you filled it out and sent it back to us last week.

"The reason most people send this card in is because they are concerned about the high cost of final expenses like burial and cremation costs, and don't want their loved ones paying the bill.

"Like I said earlier, I'm the agent that handles that in this area, and I'm here to explain how this program works.

However, I am a little curious, Mr. Prospect – when you filled

this out, what concerns did you have?" (sit back and listen).

This line of questioning allows you to establish the most important question – *The Reason Why*. This question alone will tell you why you are here, what the prospect's motivation is, and what is important to him. Once you gather the basic replies to this question, like, "I don't want to burden my loved ones with high burial costs," or, "I want to leave money to my grandson," this is where you employ the Deep Question technique, and ask the prospect, "I see what you are saying, Mr. Prospect, and why is that important to you?"

This Deep Question technique allows you to pull the emotional triggers behind the logical ones. Many of your prospects will tell you about loved ones that died without insurance, and the hardship it caused the family. These memories are painful, but emotionalizes the buying process and adds the necessary urgency to encourage a decision to be made on the stop to buy coverage today. Sometimes, however, you do not get fully-engaged responses. There are times when you need to work harder to get a more detailed response. This is where "**The 3 Question**" technique comes in handy.

The 3 Question Technique allows you to identify specifically where the client fits in his insurance situation, and allows you to pivot your sales presentation accordingly.

The 3 Question Technique Script is as follows:

"Mr. Prospect, when I meet with people who send back these

cards, typically they are in one of three situations.

The first is that they have no coverage; if they die, someone else is going to have to pay the whole thing out of pocket.

The second is they have some coverage, but not enough, as prices have gotten higher for burials.

The third situation is they have enough coverage, but want to leave money behind to loved ones, like a kid or grandkid. Tell me, Mr. Prospect, out of these 3 situations, where do you fit best?"

Once they tell you out of those three where they fit best, then you can begin to ask open-ended questions to draw out more detail. For prospects that answer that they have coverage, you will need to ask closed-ended questions like, "Who do you have your coverage with?" "How much does it cost?" "How long ago did you take your program out?" "Have you had a price increase ever?"

These fact-finding questions will allow you to determine the fundamentals of whether or not you can or need to replace the client's policy. In summary, fact-finding for final expense life insurance is elementary and simple. All the agent needs to do is determine the purpose for being there, what kind of life insurance they have, why they feel the need (if any) to own more coverage, and why that need is important to them. Once you know the facts, then you can recommend a program that meets those facts. But before you can recommend a plan based on the client's need, you need to effectively pre-qualify the client to make sure they are ready to buy today.

The Pre-Qualification Phase

Pre-qualifying your prospect is an important step in determining if a client with a need or want for your product has both (a) the health to qualify, and (b) the financial requirements to allocate towards a plan. On a broader note, the pre-qualification phase allows you to quickly assess the likelihood of selling the prospect, giving you the ability to conserve your most precious asset – **your time selling in the field.**

The transition from fact-finding to pre-qualification is to say,

"Mr. Jones, now that you've told me a lot about yourself and why you sent this card in and why it was important to you, what I want to do now is take some time to ask you some health questions.

"Whenever you look at life insurance or policies that pay for final expenses, you always want to be asked health questions because it allows you to get better coverage at a better price."

How you ask about health is up to you. I start with the birth date, I get their current age. I ask whether or not they smoke or chew tobacco within the last 12 months. Make sure you clarify, because certain carriers charge non-smoker rates for chewers or cigar smokers.

Then I ask the knockout questions:

"Do you have any kind of kidney problems, liver problems, lung problems like COPD? Do you take oxygen equipment to breathe? Ever have an organ transplant? Do you have any kind of heart problems, strokes, stents, bypasses? Seizures? Pacemaker, defibrillator? Do you take nitroglycerin? Systemic lupus, SLE? Bipolar, depression, schizophrenia? Do you have any kind of cancer ever?"

If I get a "Yes" answer to any of my questions, I ask the prospect to "Tell me more" about the condition. "When were you diagnosed?" "How long ago was it?" "How are you being treated for it now?" These questions allow you to clarify the prospect's health condition so you can choose the most suitable product for him.

That's a quick rundown of the main health questions I ask. Keep a record on how they answered it. Once you're done with those questions, conclude by asking the prospect, "OK, now what kind of prescriptions do you take? Could you go grab them so I can take a look?" After recording prescriptions, next you begin to prequalify for bank account. The way that I ask this is I say,

"Mrs. Jones, like I said, I work with a lot of different companies, and some of them give you discounts if you bank locally, if you have a bank account savings account, or go to a credit union. Do you do either of those, Mrs. Jones?"

Again, you're not saying that you're going to get a discount because of a bank. But if you look at the premium payments on policies for sending in a check versus setting up direct draft on a monthly basis, direct draft is a better price. Now you can continue forward because you know you can set up a bank draft on there. If they say no, then I just ask "Do you have one of those green Direct Express cards or use some type of debit card for your accounts?" Then they'll tell you yes or no. If they say no, you really don't have a prospect, and you can tell them right up front,

"Listen, man, most of my clients have a bank account. Most of these companies only take monthly direct draft out of your account. So you're saying you don't have anything like that, correct?"

If they say no, then you can say "You can pay quarterly, so you pay three months at a time, but I'm going to need the money today. Can you do maybe $90, $100 bucks?" I ask that because that's the minimum, and I'm not going to fool around with these people because you don't really need to waste your my time on these people.

It's very hard to sell folks without accounts, and they're not going to really show up with the money anyway 99% of the time. So my recommendation is just to be up front and see if they can pony up the money or not, before spending any longer with the prospect.

Then lastly, I sell them on premium. Meaning, once I prequalify for health, once I prequalify that they bank, I ask them the money question. The money question goes like this:

"My last question is with regards to price, and let me be totally upfront with you."

I have to be really genuine about how I say this, because I don't want to send off signals like I'm a dirty salesperson trying to take all their money. The goal behind this is to humanize you, to get them to understand that you care, that you're genuine about them and not trying to rip them off. Because they're used to that, they're seniors, people are calling them all the time trying to take their money; that's all they hear about on TV.

What I say is

"Listen, Mrs. Jones, when I sit down with people that send these cards in, 9 out of 10 people are either on Disability and draw a check because of some illness that they can't work anymore, or they're retired on Social Security. The point I'm trying to make, Mrs. Jones, is everybody that I see is on a fixed income. They really are. Again, the reason that's important is because everybody says when I sit down with them, 'I know I need final expense coverage, but I don't want to pay too much for it. It's got to fit my budget, or if it doesn't, you can just leave.'

Usually they'll laugh. But it's you being upfront with them; they appreciate that. They're surprised a salesperson would say something like that.

Then I tell them,

"The good news is, Mrs. Jones, we can make a plan that's affordable to you. We can make it fit your budget. Again, the reason that's important is the best policy to have is the one that's there when you die. It's kind of a no-brainer, right? But the one that's there when you die is the one that you can afford and you can always afford. Not the one that you've got to let go in six months and waste all your money on."

Again, asking all these really separates you from the standard salesperson, because you're making an active effort and talking about budget, trying to get them on the same page, getting them to understand that you're not there to rip them off. You're there to find something that's affordable, that's going to make sense.

Once I ask that, I ask the money question.

"Mrs. Jones, if I can qualify you for a plan – and you know your budget better than I do – you think on a monthly basis of what you can afford, can you afford somewhere between $80 to $100 a month?"

Then shut up and let them answer. You'll get several answers. Some people will say, "Oh no. No, there's no way I can afford that." Some people will say, "No, that's a little high." Some people will say,

"Depends on what you can get me." And others will say, "Yeah, that'll work."

What I do, if they say "Yeah, it'll work," I'll say,

"Hey, that's fine, Mrs. Jones. Again, we might be able to do it less, but I'm just going to use this as a starting point."

If they say, "Oh no" or any form of rejection, I say,

"Mrs. Jones, that's totally fine. Don't worry about it. The good news is it doesn't have to be that high." Then I back it down. "If I could qualify for a plan, does somewhere between $50 and $75 fit your budget?"

Then I walk it down in a stair step fashion till they can afford something. If they get to the point where they can't afford $25 to $35 bucks a month and they're 70, I'm not going to get anything for $15 bucks a month. If they're 50, I might be able to. And I'll ask them, "Can you do $15 or $10 a month?" I'll just ask them straight up.

If they can, great; if they can't, so what? *Time to pack up and see the next prospect.*

You see, **you're qualifying them**. You know their needs and wants. You get them committed to a price, too. And again, you go through all the effort of saying that you care, you're not there to rip them off for this specific reason, because you want to make sure they're on the same page.

Now if they do answer something smart, like a question to a question, like "It depends; what can you get me? Depends on what the coverage is," I always said,

"I'm not sure. I kind of have an idea, but the bottom line is, I'm going to in a minute here check and show you. But I DON'T want to quote you a policy that is way out of bounds of your price range. So it's really important to know whether or not $80 to $100 a month fits your budget. Does it?"

You need a specific answer, yes or no. Remember a "maybe" is still a "no." "Well, not really. I would probably want something less. "Let's say maybe $50, $70 a month would work?" "Yeah, that would be all right. If I can get enough coverage." At least now you've got them committed to a premium.

And this is the end of the Pre-Qualification Phase. You've asked them all the major health questions that really allow you to determine which policy is really the best to go with, so you've saved time figuring out if they're terminally ill or if they're in good shape. Then lastly, you've prequalified them based on budget and bank account.

If you're at this point, you're in a powerful position. You've asked for the information you need to determine if this really is either a suspect or a prospect. Hopefully at this point you've got a prospect, and the odds are you do if they sent this card in, and have played ball with you the entire time.

The key takeaway here is the results of your sales process gives you the basis to present a product and to confidently close on it. Because if they've given you all this information, now they're getting wide and deep in the process with you, and they're spending time with you, they're committing their feelings with you. This is after all of the stuff you've done to do the same thing: sharing who you are, sharing yourself as a human being more than just a salesperson. All the questions you've asked have been good, solid, trust, credibility-building questions. It's made a dramatic difference.

At this point, if you've got somebody who has a real reason why, somebody who has a specific, tangible purpose for having life insurance, to cover what it is they want, and then also somebody who has decent enough health and who's committed to a budget, *now you've got a prospect.* Now you can present a solution, because you've got somebody who will listen and most likely will buy.

Now, of course, nothing ever really is that smooth, so it's worthy of time to go back and make sure that we've covered the bases of pretty much everything that we've done. If we step back and we think, where can things go wrong?

You may have somebody back in the beginning who says that they've got plenty of insurance and they're just kind of curious to see what's out there. Maybe what I would call "weak prospects." They're prospects, but they're weak. You're going to have to really dig deeper and ask tougher questions to really determine if it's worth your time spending with somebody.

Because the fact is, if somebody can't verbalize the reason why they sent it in or if they've got really weak reasons and you can't build upon it, you really don't have a prospect; you've got a suspect, and you need to leave as fast as possible.

I employ the **devil's advocate technique**. The devil's advocate technique is a to the point, straightforward, question, that determines whether or not I've got a prospect. I turn around the situation on a prospect. What I mean by devil's advocate question is if I have somebody who says, "Yeah, I've got a $100,000 policy," and let's say I've done a policy review on it and it's a whole life policy. It's a good policy and they're paying really cheap for it; they've had it for 50 years.

I'm going to ask,

"Well, Mrs. Jones, listen, you're smart. I really mean it. Very few people that I see that send these cards in have as much insurance as you do. You've done a really good job, and trust me, when you see so many people that ignore insurance, it's commendable to see people who actually care and want to protect their loved ones.

"Which kind of leads me to my question; honestly, you've got enough for burial, you've got enough to pay for final expenses – more than enough to pay for final expenses. What would be your

reason for having any more than what you have right now?"

Some agents think, "Oh my gosh, I can't believe you're asking that question. You're trying to talk yourself out of a deal." But what you're doing here is asking a fading question, allowing them to come forth and tell the reasons why they can be sold.

You'll get people who say, "Well, I really don't see any reasons to have any more" or "Yeah, I guess I've got enough." Then I'll clarify and say, "Does that mean there's really no reason to be even looking at adding any more coverage?" Or you'll get somebody who says, "Yeah, I really want to leave this to my loved ones and I don't want this to go to the funeral home and spend $20,000 of it." Because the fact is, every prospect has unique reasons why to buy, and you want to give them the opportunity to tell why.

Very often in this particular line of business, you're going to sell people who have a specific need, and you want to know what that need is. And I want to know it quickly, especially if the odds are this particular prospect doesn't really have a need. And that's okay if he doesn't. You just want to save your time and not go through a pitch if unnecessary in the first place.

Another section that I like to cover is the policy review stage.

Very important, especially if you're brand new. You can do this in the beginning, when you ask the three questions we spoke of earlier, or you can do this anywhere in the prequalification stage.

If they say they've got coverage, you always want to ask, "Who do you have coverage with? Do you mind if I ask who you've got coverage with?" Mostly they'll tell you. "Foresters, Mutual of Omaha, Colonial Penn." Then I ask, "How much coverage have you got, and if you don't mind me asking, what are you paying for it?" Then you've got all the facts. And "How long have you had the policy?" That's enough to make a determination about where they stand.

Once you're experienced in this, you'll know, especially if it's a Colonial Penn or Mutual of Omaha, that they've got a policy that's graded for the first two years, and if they just picked it up, odds are they don't realize that and that they're going to have to get through two years before they're actually covered. This is a lay-down sale, because once you find that, it's easy; you just go in there and you can replace the bad boy with full coverage on the first day. So it's really important that you see the policy and check it out.

Now, you'll have some people who have these exotic policies that you've never heard of like Conseco, etc., known as flexible premium or universal life insurance programs. Typically these policies have price increases and cancel at future dates. It's a little more detailed in explaining, but basically, if you see one of those, many times the premiums aren't fixed. Unless it says the premiums are guaranteed forever, most of the time they're guaranteed for a particular number of years and then it's totally based on the cash value of the policy, whether they go up or not.

And the way that you know if it's universal life is they'll tell you "It's like $20 bucks a month, I've got $50,000 in coverage." Then you ask them, "Does your policy cancel? Does it go up?" and they'll say, "No, the agent said it was whole life and I've had it since the '80s and early '90s."

Asking the tough questions are tough

Agents occasionally bemoan that these are the "tough questions" they want to avoid and wait until the end of the sales call to ask. My perspective is different. Asking the tough questions saves the agent and the prospect time, and allows you to spend more time finding the true prospects that have the ability, need, and urgency to buy.

After training hundreds of final expense agents, I have found most severely shorten or altogether ignore this most critical part of the presentation, usually because they are afraid to ask tough questions.

As mentioned above, implementing and committing to this section of the presentation will afford you more time to find the good prospects to sell to while simultaneously reducing your frustration level pitching to unqualified prospects.

Final Expense Sales Presentation And Figuring Out The "Why" Is Of Utmost Importance

I had a call-in yesterday from a new agent on a final expense sales presentation call. She's actually quite experienced in the business, but she had a prospect that had a specific condition that would make him almost un-insurable, besides a few guaranteed issue companies.

I had the pleasure of eavesdropping on the conversation and listened how she approached and sold this particular prospect. The prospect gave her the ultimatum type objection, meaning "it's either $100 for $10K or nothing," which truly was impossible to achieve. As I was listening to the conversation, going back and forth between pricing, options, what we can do, what can't happen, etc., it dawned on me that I didn't understand what the whole purpose of the meeting was.

You see, the way I teach how final expense sales presentations work is that the 'why' is the most important factor that determines whether or not your lead is worth selling final expense.

When you're in a home delivering a final expense sales presentation, you need to know EXACTLY why this person is even having you over. What is his motivation? What do they want to accomplish? If you don't know, you can easily progress through a final expense sales presentation and then "lose" it, wondering what the heck happened!

The truth is that a lot of times when you "lose" a prospect in a final expense sales presentation, you never really "had" them and it's usually because of something you didn't ask or get clarification on.

Turns out as you could imagine, this particular agent had not asked the "why" questions so critical to the sales process. It was obvious; I didn't hear it per say, but they were dabbling over minor stuff that didn't really cover the underlying reason why the lead would even consider buying final expense burial insurance in the first place. On the phone with my agent, I backed up and asked, "What's this guy's situation?" And she said, "He's got some insurance and wants more." I said, "Well, how much does the guy have?" She said, "He's got $25K in life insurance coverage." I asked her, "Well what is the reason he would like more?" The agent said the lead wanted to have more, he believes in it. To me, that alone is NOT enough of a reason why. Why? The reason is not clear, it's not specific, and it's not backed by any kind of urgency or demand. Sometimes you can make sales regardless of that, but nevertheless, at the end of the day we're talking about a situation in which this particular prospect didn't have an underlying need. In most business situations, we have to negotiate a win-win scenario. And giving final expense sales presentations is no different. While the lead may be able to get the price he wants, he may have to cut back on coverage a little to do it.

In the end, this agent's lead did not want to negotiate a win-win deal. He wouldn't listen to reason. He wouldn't listen to the other side of the story, but the truth is even listening to reason and the other side of the story, the agent didn't take the time to understand where that prospect was coming from in the beginning.

Had she done that, she may have realized very early on that this person truly had no reason to even be involved in a final expense sales presentation in the first place. There are situations when you do these kinds of final expense sales presentations, and you employ 'the devil's advocate' line of questioning. Most people don't spend more money than they need to on life insurance if they don't need it, as it's ultimately a product that really never realizes any kind of immediate gratification.

I'm gone if the guy doesn't fall into my trap, so to speak, and that's why the devil's advocate approach when giving a final expense sales presentation is so great. It allows the prospect to sell YOU on why I should sell him, and it gives you the cue to get on with your business and go see somebody who's actually a prospect. That's my whole approach on why asking the 'why' is the most important part of the final expense sales presentation. Having a satisfactory response to 'why you need this' is what matters the most and if you don't get one, you don't have a prospect and it's time to move on.

Final Expense Sales Training Part 3: Presenting Final Expense To A Prospect.

Once you've taken the time to pre-qualify the prospect, **how do you present final expense life insurance in a way that persuades the prospect to buy today?**

The good news is that if you have gotten to this point, and followed the steps outlined, odds are the prospect has an underlying need and ability to buy final expense burial insurance. Even better, he most likely respects you as a final expense life insurance professional, and will most likely buy from you if you can demonstrate what you do is obviously a benefit to the prospect. Luckily in the final expense business, there are many inferior life insurance products, and **your goal is to clearly compare and contrast what the competition offers to what you offer, factually showing the prospect how what you sell is of superior value.**

Agents should be trained on how to show prospects what the mail order and television commercials offering burial insurance hide in the fine print. Simply showing them the facts is usually enough to emotionally bother the client enough that he see no value in buying from your competition. Once you establish the facts of the competitions' shortcomings, that is when the final expense agent demonstrates what makes his burial insurance product different and clearly more beneficial.

The presentation is fact-focused and does not rely upon hard-sell tactics. Honestly, agents will see no need to hard-sell, assuming they can effectively communicate and show the prospect the inferiority of the competitions' life insurance products while demonstrably showing why the agents' final expense burial insurance products are superior. Selling this way is called "consultative selling," and you are seen as the advocate for the prospect's best interest, taking the time to educate the prospect on his options. Consultative selling in the presentation is where real rapport is built, which is what truly closes the sell.

The Presentation

Let's describe and discuss how to make a case for why you sell what you sell and why it's important for the qualified prospect to buy today.

At this point, you absolutely need to have complete compliance on the previous sections. You don't give a presentation to somebody who's not interested or doesn't fit the terms of qualifying. Having an unqualified prospect is like the saying, "The Living Dead." It doesn't make any sense! Point is you don't have a true prospect. Therefore there's no need to do a presentation, right? So spend less time being frustrated. Give presentations only to people that fit the profile of what is a prospect. Anything else short of a true prospect is not one which you should waste any time on.

Now we're into the actual presentation of our product and describing why the prospect should do business with us today. That's important to understand. The key word in that sentence is "**today**." You want under no uncertain terms, at the end of the presentation, to ask for the business at the end. We'll get more to the specifics of the close, but it's absolutely fundamental that you actually get the business today.

You do all that following these techniques. At this point in the presentation, there's different ways to present a solution to the need

to the prospect. I have a particular way that I enjoy, which makes sense, but in my opinion, it basically eliminates any other options out there. You see, you have to think how a prospect would think. First of all, if you've set an appointment or you've door knocked them, you have to think as skeptically as possible.

Imagine some salesperson you don't know comes into your home and introduces himself. He sounds nice, he sounds credible. You as a prospect don't want to get a bad deal. So you're thinking in the back of your head, "I'm going to look around and see if I can buy somewhere else" or "I want to make sure that this guy is trustworthy. I'm not going to buy today." They're thinking that as you're talking to them.

The most important factor is that you must expect skepticism and objections, and must design your presentation to knock out those concerns ahead of time. You've done that with your prequalification routine, but you also are going to need to do that when it comes to demonstrating how your product is different and better than the alternative. I employ a couple of different tactics to do this. And you'll hear them intertwined within the presentation.

The first of which is an **apples to oranges comparison**. What I mean by that is in the presentation, we're going to compare products that are out there that are not an apples to apples comparison. But for the purpose of how we frame our argument, we want to compare what we offer to the junkiest alternatives available.

What that's going to do is (a), establish more credibility because you know what's out there. People are going to understand and see, "Hey, this agent knows what's out there. He's abreast of the information." They may not necessarily think this, but it's going to be an unconscious process that they'll get.

And (b), it establishes your product in the light that is most favorable to the consumer. If you really think about how an insurance product works, you've got A. M. Best ratings, you have customer service, you have terms of conditioning, fraternal benefit organizations versus insurance companies. You have all different variations of things that make up an insurance company. "Insurance company" is really a tip of the iceberg expression or definition. Everybody sells life insurance, but as we all know, life insurance and the factors that influence is credibility and positioning is not always the same.

So the reason I'm going through this detailed explanation is that with an apples to oranges comparison, you're going to look at the main factors that make these companies sellable or unsellable. You're going to draw that comparison to yours. In the end, it's going to be completely obvious your product or solution is superior, compared to your other options.

Also, I believe a presentation should be interactive. You want to have engagement. You want them to be a part of the process of your presentation. If they're not, then they will pull away and miss vital points, deciding not to buy from you because they'll be confused. So I always ask questions at the close. I call it **trial closing.** I ask for their opinion on what works best for them. And I let them tell me why. So I don't really even sell them. They hear in their own words, in their own expressions and tonality why a product is superior over the other.

When somebody sells themselves, it's a much stronger sale and you're going to close a lot more that way as opposed to pushing them into a product.

Now, here is the transition from Pre-Qualification to Presentation:

"Mr. Prospect, now that you've told me all that you have, my question to you is this: there's a lot of different life insurance programs out there. I know you get all sorts of stuff in the mail

and see it on TV. For the purpose of describing how my product works versus the others, do you know the difference between term life insurance and whole life insurance?"

You'll get a variety of answers, most of the time which are "No, I don't know the difference" or "No, I have no clue." And that's good because now you've taken the role of an expert, who is in the best interest of the prospect. After I ask them that, assuming they say no,

I answer that question saying,

"That's all right, Mrs. Jones. Most people I talk to have no clue what the difference is.

"The reason I bring it up is because I want you to choose the best choice of which type of insurance to have because they're not all the same. Some are better than the others. But you need to know the facts to make a sound decision that's right for you and your family."

Most of the time they'll shake their head in agreement because that makes sense. Of course, the prospect needs to know all the facts before making a decision. How can you argue with that? Additionally, this question lends you credibility because you show respect to the prospect's buying criteria. The first thing that I do is go right into the term portion of the presentation. I say,

"Mrs. Jones, let me start with term insurance. Have you ever

heard of AARP or Globe Life Insurance?"

Everybody will say yes. What I've done in my presentation now is I've taken a laminated letter that AARP sends out. These people, you have to understand, get two or three letters a week from either AARP or Globe or some other insurance company so this all will have some level of familiarity to them, which increases your credibility. I pull out a laminated page that describes a product, and I've highlighted certain areas on the sales letter that tells how the product works. I'll tell them,

"Mrs. Jones, this is AARP's letter they send out to you, you get in the mail. If you see where it's highlighted at the top, it says this is group level term life insurance. Here's the thing: whenever you see the word 'term' in any kind of insurance letter, that means the policy will terminate at a certain age."

Most people, again, connecting term and terminate, it's going to make an easier mind connection. Most people are like "Really?" Then I say,

"Go ahead and flip it over and read it for yourself. If you see where it's highlighted, it says the insurance is good up to age 80. What they don't tell you is what happens after age 80? What happens is that you lose all your insurance, no matter how much money you put in. They keep the money and you get no benefit.

"So the question you have to ask yourself, Mrs. Jones, is are

you planning on kicking the bucket before or after 80?"

That usually elicits a little response. Sometimes it's serious.

"But the point is, now you can make the connection, who would want insurance – you may live past 80; a lot of people are, even with medications, even in a nursing home. The average age is going above 80 each and every passing year. The point is, why would you want insurance that may cancel before you go?"

Then I go onto say:

"To make matters worse, they actually raise their prices every three to five years. What happens is they get you in cheap, but as you get older and as your income becomes more fixed, they raise their prices. Then what happens is most people actually don't outlive it; they cancel it because they can't afford it."

At that point, they're like "yeah," then ask them, "What do you think about that?" Most people say, "I don't want anything like this."

A lot of these people are handing you back saying "I don't want this junk." But once you ask them "What's your thoughts about that? What do you think about that?" if they haven't told you, they're like, "Yeah, it's a bunch of junk. Why would anybody want this?" That's the kind of response you want.

And then you say, **"Yeah, absolutely. Most people don't realize how bad these are until they see it for themselves. "So that's term** life; it cancels and the rates increase.

"Now I'm going to show you something called guaranteed acceptance life insurance."

At that point, I hand them another letter and I say,

"Have you ever seen the TV commercials about Colonial Penn with the Jeopardy guy, Alex Trebek?" Most people say "Yeah, I remember them. Oh yeah, absolutely." What I tell them is this: I say, "Listen, the way they pitch their product is they've got a bunch of ladies around in some cafeteria, and they say you don't ask any health questions, you're immediately approved, and it sounds great, everybody's smiling, patting each other on the back, blah blah blah. But they don't ask any health questions, but they approve you for coverage. It kind of sounds a little fishy, doesn't it, at least?"

"What's the catch?" is what most people think.

Here's what I do. I show them the letter, I say, "Check out in the fine print where it's highlighted," and then I read it out to them.

I say,

"You understand that this product is a modified death benefit program where the payout is reduced during the first two years of non-accidental death." I tell them "What that means in real language, real terms, is that this policy does not pay anything if

you die from natural causes – strokes, heart attacks, anything like that within the first two years."

Then I go into more description. I say, "**Mrs. Jones, if you make**

it to the 23rd month of the 27th day and you die of a heart attack, it doesn't matter if you're just that close to two years; this thing ain't paying out. They just give your money back and a little bit of interest. If you had a $5,000 policy, might only get $500. Is that enough to pay for a burial?" They'll say no. "Or cremation?" No.

And then I go into catching them off guard. I say, "**This is a perfect product for people who don't qualify for anything else. But the fact is, you're in great shape. You may have had some health issues, but it's not a problem now, and the truth is there's so many other insurance companies that will take you Day 1 coverage, immediate, and give you even a better price than what Colonial Penn has.**"

At that point, I've shown them why this is bad and I've described it to them. Sometimes I'll also say it's like the reverse of term. You have to pray that you'll live another two years before you're really, truly covered. "Do you want to do that? Does that make sense to you?" Most people say, "No, that's junk, too."

The point is you're getting them engaged, painting pictures of what these plans do for people. Once you're experienced in the pitch, you can start adding stories you've collected in the field. You'll eventually run across people that have these products, and what you can start doing is just saying, "Hey, I was seeing Rosie up in Hixson and the same thing happened. She had a Colonial Penn policy, had no idea." Or,"She had a friend who had a Colonial Penn policy and died in the 12th month; she thought she had $10,000 coming for her daughter, and her daughter was shocked to find out that Colonial Penn only had to pay out what she paid in, which was basically $1,000. Not near enough to pay for a funeral, and that was all they had. They had to go to church, friends."

Paint the picture. See the hearse backed up against the door, the embarrassment of it. That's what you have to do, and then when you can start putting in those testimonials, it becomes that much more powerful. At that point, once I've described that, I say

"Let me show you how mine works. I do what's called senior final expense whole life insurance. There's three main benefits to how my program is better than what the other two are, #1, the rates never increase."

With these three benefits, I would phrase it in a way where the last one you hit is the one that you feel is the most important to them, and you can kind of develop a sense for that. But either way, you're going to find out what it is, and I'll show you how to do that in a second.

"The main benefit, #1, is the rates never increase. Your

payments are locked from the very first day that you take it out to your final day on earth. There's never a rate increase, ever, guaranteed, end of story.

"The second benefit of the product is that it never cancels because of age or health. So it lasts the rest of your life; it never cancels for any other reason except if you miss a payment if you don't make payments. But if your health changes, you get to be 120, you still have coverage.

"Then lastly, your coverage is Day 1 100% coverage."

This is assuming you've got a prospect that fits your health. You might have somebody who kind of does, and his coverage may be graded coverage where you get 30% first year, 70% second year. Just modify the pitch, because it's still better than nothing.

"The final thing is that this is Day 1 100% coverage from the very first day. The reason I mention that is so important is because of your health, it qualifies you for immediate protection. Just say, God forbid, something does happen in the first two years. It's going to give you the peace of mind you said you wanted and not burden your loved ones, your daughter, with a burial."

Then also, I'll mention a couple other things.

"You choose the beneficiaries; if you want your daughter to as the beneficiary, that's no problem. It pays out 100% accidental

death and natural death coverage, so however you go, it pays."

Then I summarize it: **"It's what you see is what you get product. You know what you're going to pay, you know it's never going up, you know it lasts as long as you do no matter what age you live, and you're covered from the first day for the full amount.**

At this point, I use a sales technique called the "let the prospect hang themselves" technique. I trial close them on the concept. I want them buying into my idea, and I want them to tell me they buy into it without me forcing it out of them.

So what I do is I ask them the question: **"Mrs. Jones, now that we've looked through all of these programs and now that you've seen the facts and actual options for what's out there, out of the three, the term that cancels, guaranteed acceptance that really doesn't cover you for two years, or mine, where you're covered immediately and your rates stay the same and it's covered forever, which one do you feel works best for you?"** And sit back and wait.

Ninety-nine out of 100 of them are going to say, "Well duh, yours is better." And I say, "Yeah, I know." Or you say something like,

"Yeah, it's a no-brainer, right? Why would you want something where you don't have the guarantees in place that are so important? It just doesn't make any sense."

Pretty much everybody I meet with says the exact same thing. Again, relating it to the group en masse; you're not alone in this decision. You're demonstrating to them the facts that this is a good idea because everybody else says so too. At that point, what I do is now I ask them, **"What do you like about the program the best?"**

"Oh, I like the fact that it's" – and they'll tell you. Again, this is why the hanging themselves comes in. I want to hear them say it. In my opinion, if you can have somebody who can verbally tell you with their own words what they like about what you are selling, it engenders and commits them more to you and what you have to offer. It lets you know what they think is most important.

Final Expense Sales Training Part 4: Closing and Handling Objections

Closing the sale should be the easiest element of your presentation.

Why? Because if you properly followed the other steps of the presentation, by now, the prospect is qualified, has a need, has a budget, and has urgency; all the close consists of is asking for the business! The closing phraseology suggested for final expense agents in a sales process is the assumptive close, where the agent shows three price points and three corresponding coverage amounts.

All the agent needs to say is, "Here are the three programs you qualify for; which fits your budget best?" After that, simply stay quiet until the prospect decides. It may take a few seconds for them to talk. There maybe a little bit of awkward silence. Do not speak until they say something (very important)! Ninety percent of the time, the prospect will choose a program without objection, assuming you properly followed the system to a tee.

What happens if you do get objection?

Most objections have to do with pricing, meaning it's too expensive. So let's discuss how to handle that. Most of the time, the objection starts with, "Let me think about it." When I hear that, I reiterate what they said to be clear, then ask them, **"When you say**

you need to think about it, how do you mean?" Then I stay quiet until I hear an adequately expressed explanation.

This is where they'll say something about pricing. Again, once they express themselves, then I ask, **"Besides the price, is there anything else that is preventing you from making a decision today?"** This is called "Isolating the Objection" now that you know the true objection is price, you can begin to work on it.

This is where I employ the **"Something is Better than Nothing"** rebuttal, explaining that the prospect's family would prefer a little bit of coverage versus nothing. The idea behind the rebuttal is to rationalize why starting with less than the desired amount is better for everyone involved.

Sometimes, objections are stall-tactics made by weak-willed people to try to get you to go away. From the perspective of an actual producer, if the prospect can't be forthright with you - especially after you have been forthright, honest, and transparent - most likely the person across the table from you is a low-life, time-wasting, agent-killer. I find ending the sales call the most effective solution to deal with people who can't honestly express themselves. As a new agent, you must carefully plan and analyze your sales process and make sure you are following the system closely so as to ensure you are not missing steps that cause the objections at the end. Nevertheless, no salesperson closes every appointment, and some of the best salespeople in the final expense industry making six-figures and more have three out of every four leads tell them they are not interested.

The takeaway here is to focus on developing your presenting and pre-qualifying skills above all else. And while you need to understand how to close, certainly do not expend too much energy beyond the basics, as the sale is made early on in the appointment, not at the end. Assuming the prospect chooses a plan, I say,

"That's fine, Mrs. Jones. At this point, let me look through my book here and show you what I have. Let's see what works best." If you haven't mentioned it already – I mention it in the beginning, but I used to mention it in the end – I say, "Mrs. Jones, one more thing I need to tell you: I'm what's known as a broker in this business. Do you know what that means?" They usually say, "Maybe, I don't know." I say, "Most agents you'll run into are married to one company, like All State, State Farm." Again, mention one that everybody's heard of. "They can only offer the product that that company has, nothing else. Problem is, a lot of these companies are not flexible on coverage and charge a higher price than what's really competitive.

"What I do is I actually have access to them all." When you say you have "access to all final expense companies," that doesn't mean you are appointed with all of them. It just means you have the accessibility to appoint with whomever you choose.

"That means I can shop around, see which program works best for you, and give you the one that's going to give you the best quality coverage at the best possible, most competitive price."

Most people at that point say, "Oh, that's cool. Okay." So now they know, now you've knocked out that "I'm going to shop around" objection because you've looked at all the prices. And if you are a broker, you know where pricing stands with different final expense carriers. It's so much easier to be convicted in that approach because you really do represent them all and you can **sell the program** that makes sense. At that point what I do is I tell them, "Give me a few minutes here, let me see what works best." So I'll look through there. I already have a pretty good idea. I may make some behavioral gestures demonstrating I am not picking the first carrier I see. Then at that point I say,

"Mrs. Jones, here is the best program you qualify for." I hand them a brochure and then I say **"This company's name is ABC Life Insurance Company."**

I always mention their A.M. Best rating and then I also mention their years in service. I explain to them that the A. M. Best rating is basically a financial auditor that looks at life insurance companies' financials and gives a grade, so consumers know if this company's managing money well, or if it's going broke. Then I go on to say,

"The program you qualify for is Immediate Solution Program, whatever the name of the specific product is," and I'll tell them, **"and it's exactly just like I described earlier."** This is where I hit up what matters the most.

"Like I said, the coverage lasts forever; the rates never go up, and like what you said was most important to you, what you liked about it best is that it's a Day 1 100% coverage. You are covered immediately from the time you take this policy out and it goes into force. So again, you never have to worry about having the uncertainty of being covered, like you would with the other ones."

Then at this point, I transition into asking the health questions. I always recommend new agents do this to assure yourself you're picking the right carrier. What I do at this point is I ask them the health questions. I say, **"I just want to make sure 100% I can qualify you."** Again, really important for newbies because you may have overlooked a minor health issue; this way, you're saving time. And it's always safe to go backtrack anyway. They're not going to hold it against you if you go to another product line instead. I'll ask them, word for word all the health questions and let them know either answer yes or no. Once I'm done, I say, "Yes, you definitely qualify."

What I do now is I take the price range they gave me and I give them a good, better, best price. What that does is it allows me to show the low side of the range, the medium side, and the higher prices. It just gives them the opportunity to pick the one that they like the best that makes the most sense. Next, I will say, "Let me go ahead and run some numbers here," so I'll run some numbers and I'll write them on a paper – usually the back of the card or copy of the card that they sent in. I'll say, **"Mr. Jones, based on your age and health, here's what we can do for the range that you gave me."**

What I do is I try to reiterate it back to the facts they gave me.

"Mr. Jones, you want to be buried and leave a little money behind. I'm completely confident that any of these plans are going to do that. My suggestion is to pick the one that fits your budget the best. They're all going to do the job, but you want to do the one that just really makes the most sense.

"So which one of these programs would work best for you?" is how you close.

You are NOT asking them, "Are you going to buy, yes or no?" You are asking, **"Which one works best?"** It's assumed that they're going to buy. The assumption close is the most common close to use in life insurance sales. It's the most effective close across all sorts of industries. Ask them which one they prefer to do.

So hopefully, if you've done your job well, you've prequalified,

you've demonstrated the presentation effectively, you've built credibility and rapport, you've trial closed them, they feel firm about the decision of which one works best for them, you shouldn't really get any objections at this point. But everybody does get objections, and there's always a way to handle those basic objections. At this point, if you get the nod, you go through and fill out the application, if you do a phone interview, make sure you tell them what to expect on the phone interview.

"They're going to ask for all your information like I did and then they're going to ask you health questions, same ones. Just answer them truthfully. They may ask you some questions about prescription medications in the end, and if they do, just answer truthfully. And then we'll know in about 10 to 15 minutes that you're approved and we'll know that you are totally approved, no issues. Does that sound fair?"

And then ask "Do you have any other questions or concerns?" Just reiterate, "Don't worry about it, don't be stressed out about it. It's real straightforward and easy." But let's assume now we're going getting some resistance and objections. The most common objections that you'll hear in this business are "I can't afford it today," "I need to think about it" – which again is a smokescreen, which we'll get into later.

You might hear some "I don't want to put it on my bank account" or "I don't want to put it on my Direct Express card objections." There's ways around that. That's more along the lines of just being new and not establishing enough credibility.

But the one that you'll hear about is "I can't afford it today." If you get that, just say, "That's fine because I don't even take checks most of the time anyway. I set it up to bill later." I don't say I set it up to bank draft later because that may be an objection later, a new objection you have to get over.

At this point, they're not necessarily qualified and it might halt the entire process. So just say "We set it up to bill later." It's just a quick and easy way to get the point across that they don't have to give you money. Another common is "Let me think about it. I don't do anything the first day," there's a really simple approach to counter this common objection, which really is good for any objection. The most common way that I counter resistance or objections is I always rebuttal with,

"Okay, I understand what you're saying, but could you tell me a little bit of how do you mean? What exactly do you mean, you need to think about it?" And just be quiet. Let them tell you and let them take the time to express themselves. And you'll hear all sorts of things like money objections, like "I need to talk to my kids" objections. This is where you get really to the objections themselves. If it's a money objection, tell them, **"So what you're saying, Mrs.**

Jones, is that the numbers I've showed you, they're out of your budget. Yes or no?" And they'll say "yes." "That's fine, Mrs. Jones. Let me show you some less expensive ones."

What I do when I get the money objection or it's too expensive objection, I say **"Listen, Mrs. Jones, if you think it's out of your budget, that's fine. The thing is, isn't some coverage better than none?"** is what I'll ask them. Most times they'll say "Yeah, I'd say so." If they say, "Well, it depends," I'll say, **"Listen Mrs. Jones, if your daughter finds you dead, she's been on money problems, and you had the choice to take even a smaller policy out for $5,000 or nothing for $0 because you didn't want to deal with it, do you think she's going to have resentment towards you at that point?"**

What that allows you to do is to show something smaller. If you showed the $60 to $80 and they give you resistance, show them $35, $45, $55. Rewrite it and say "Which one works best for you?" Just go right back into the close on the money question and let them see. That's the big one that you'll hear if you didn't properly, thoughtfully go through prequalifying for the money earlier on in the presentation.

If you hear a "Let me think about it" and you've done all of this in the past, again, the question is, "That's fine, Mrs. Jones. I'm just curious, when you say 'I need to think about it,' what do you mean specifically?" That will open up other things. A lot of the times, buyers are liars, and you're not necessarily going to get the entirety of the reason why somebody's objecting, but what happens is that it's going to allow you to get to the reasons why somebody would resist. And most of the time, what it comes down to is money or need and the things that the entire presentation really should have handled from the beginning.

I don't get very many objections. If I do, it's these strange conditions that really don't make any sense. Well, make sense, but necessarily aren't true objections. "I'm completely broke." Usually, you find that out in the end. Or whatever. So the thing is, if you get a lot of resistance, the key thing to approach any objection is, **"I understand what you're saying, but could you please tell me specifically how you mean 'I need to think about it'?"**

Let them tell you the reasons, and once you know the reasons, say, "Is there any other reason besides this – money, talk to kids, that you wouldn't take out a policy today?" Then let them tell you yes or no. Get all the objections. Once they say no, then say **"Mrs. Jones, if there is a way to get you something that fits your budget, or if there is a way to get your kids buying on this today, would you have any reason not to move forward? Would you be ready to move forward and get the coverage that you told me in the beginning you wanted?"**

What you're doing now is you're rationally dissecting the objections, any that are out there, and then trial closing again on the idea, "Now can we move forward dependent upon that?" If they're going to say no, then they're not worth your time. They're going to be pussy-footing around and you need to get out of there. There's probably something you missed way early on that you overlooked or glossed over. Again, happens to us all. We waste our time with non-prospects.

What happens at this point is that if it's a money problem just say, **"Hey listen, that's not a problem, because we can do less than this amount of money. Let me show you what I can do."** Or if it's a kids problem, say, **"Hey Mrs. Jones, most people that I have as prospects or have as clients, they say the same thing. A lot of people say the same thing as you. I understand. You want your kids to be a part of this. But the bottom line truth is that do you feel there would be any objection by your children to have anything like this?"** It's probably one of the most difficult objections.

Point Of Sale Phone Interview Prep

In final expense, there are a lot of different carriers out there, most of which require a point of sale interview. What that means is when you're in the house of the prospect, the idea behind it is that you can prequalify immediately and then when you leave the house, you've got somebody who's approved – pre-approved, at least – and you're not going to have to go back and forth, chasing China eggs or trying to make something out of nothing. So this allows you to be more efficient.

I recommend this wholeheartedly to new agents to do and pick carriers that do point of sale interviews. It takes extra time, but you want to do things right, not quickly in this business. Especially when you start off, because you will forget things; you won't remember all of the different details. You'll go through an underwriting point of sale and you forgot to ask about prescriptions or something, whereas if you walked out of the house with an app that did not require point of sale and then they initiate a randomized phone interview or ask you to go back and clarify things, it's just going to eat your time up.

So long story short, short of specific recommendations on carriers to use, because that's always in flux and changing, I do definitely recommend picking your initial carriers as having one that require and have you do a point of sale interview. It's that important. It just makes your life easier in the long run, once you invest the 10 to 15 minutes. That's really all it takes to do the phone interview.

What I do, after I qualify and get them to pick the program they want, what I do is I ask them who do they want to be their beneficiary. This allows them to think, who do they want to receive the lump sum payment? Then I get into the specifics. If I need to clarify their name, we just do all the regular housekeeping stuff; name, address, city/state, Social Security number, date of birth, so on and so forth. I just go through all that.

At that point I say, **"Listen Mr. Jones, I'm going to take you through what to expect on this particular phone call." Before I get to this, I'll just run through the health questions one last time.**

I'll ask it word-for-word and make sure that they totally qualify, and just to make sure I didn't miss anything." Again, very important is to double and triple check as a new agent and make sure that everything checks out.

Now moving to the phone interview preparation. You don't want to do the phone interview for them, nor do you want to coach them through a phone interview, but what you do want to do is prepare them for what to expect. What my script is when I talk to a person and we're prepping them for the phone interview, I say, **"Mrs. Jones, here's what's going to happen next. You're pre-approved for coverage based on the questions I asked you, and what we're going to do now is just do a 10-minute phone interview to go ahead and qualify you for sure over the phone, so that way when I leave, I know that you definitely are approved for coverage."**

At this point, 99 out of 100 times you will not get an objection. If you get an objection, just sell the phone interview like "It'll be real quick; get it over with. It's not a big deal." What you're going to say at that point is, **"Just to make sure that you're totally onboard with what's going to happen, let me tell you what to expect. I'm going to call them; I'm going to give them my information, tell them who I am, my agent number, all that stuff. Once they're done with me, I'll hand the phone to you and what's going to happen is that they're going to confirm the same information I asked you. Then they're going to ask if you've been read or you understand that**

you're going to have an MIB prescription history check done over the phone. It's some long language. Once you hear that, if you agree, say 'Yes, I agree.'"

Again, most point of sale interviews ask for basically a "verbal" signature, so again, you want to prep them and just say "This is just what everybody does. They have a health history check over the phone, they see it on the database, just to make sure everybody checks out," so again, they're not going to be alarmed, "What are you talking about?" Some of them have fraud statements; just say, "Hey, they're going to ask about the fraud statement, that you are aware of it. That's just telling them that you're not committing fraud and you understand the consequences. Just say 'Yes, I agree' if you agree."

Then you go through to the end, and then you say, **"At this point, this is when they ask about whether or not you've smoked or chewed tobacco or used tobacco in the past 12 months, depending on how the application says. If that's true that you have not used it, say no. Then they'll ask about your height and weight; give them that. Then when you actually get to the health questions, they ask you the same health questions I asked you just a moment ago. So assuming everything you said was true, say the same exact yes or no answer. If you've answered everything no, just say no. You don't have to give additional information. Just a simple 'no' is all that's necessary based on how the questions are worded."**

"Once you get to the end, typically they'll have you hand the phone to me and give me the approval. They may have questions about prescriptions. They'll tell you they're going to do a prescription check. So be prepared; they may ask about prescriptions you currently use or you used in the past. Answer it the best you can, and when they ask for date of use, give the best date of use you can. Just do the best you can to answer it. Doesn't mean you're not going to get qualified; they just ask a lot of these questions anyway. Do you have any questions? Anything like that? Okay, perfect."

So that's all you say. And then I dial the number and we go through the process.

Wrapping Up And Cooling Down The Presentation

At this point, we've discussed walking through and getting the person qualified over the phone for the point of sale interview. This next section concerns wrapping up and cooling down the presentation. We do this because we need to make sure that the policy is double and triple sold, so the prospect won't call the next day and decide to cancel it. We also do a cool down and rap up to create lasting positive impression with the new client, so as to protect your new business from getting replaced by other agents that come in behind you. The last piece of business that one must take care of is how are we going to have this policy paid. The reason I place payment at the very end is because one of the conditions of doing business.

If you **mention early on you** bank draft before you've established the benefits of what you do, you can throw a monkey wrench in into the sales process. I save the bank draft question for the end because when you discuss bank drafts and payment methods at the end, they've already spent the last hour and a half with you going through the motions, seeing what they qualify for, doing everything that's necessary in order to put the policy into force. The whole point of me doing this is that they've already invested a good portion of the time and there really isn't any other reason at this point but to just go ahead and follow through with it because hopefully at this point I've done enough and we've conversed enough that they trust me, know that I'm legitimate, and they're going to do business. It's just too much time to go through another presentation, so just why not do it this one time?

My exact script that I use when I'm sitting across the table after I qualify them, I say,

"Mr. Jones, last little bit of business that we need to do is just figure out when and how to set up payment. I just want to tell you upfront, we don't expect any payment today. It's not required. What everybody does is sets it up to bill for the following month. When do you usually get paid? Most people set it up when they get paid. Mr. Jones, when do you typically get your check?" At this point, they're going to say, "Oh, on the 3rd, on the second

Wednesday."

At that point, once I get that, I say,

"Okay, the third. Typically most people in those situations set it up for the 4th or the 5th. Which day would be best for you to set up a bank draft for that day, starting next month?"

I don't ask them if you would like to set up a bank draft; I tell them, "Which day would you prefer to set up a bank draft?" So you've assumed the bank draft close. They will tell you at that point which they prefer. 99% of the time, it's not a big deal. Sometimes it is. They'll let you know. But what I do at that point, assuming there's no objections, is just go ahead and get them to sign it, write it down, and then we've got that important part taken care of.

If you get objections like "Does it have to be on bank draft?" or kind of milk-toasty, weak objections, that's okay. That's your opportunity to say, **"Listen, Mr. Jones, yes, you do, and the reason is this: none of these companies will set up any other form of payment just because it costs a lot to mail, it's a hassle to chase people down, and the bottom line is it's better for you because it's predictable, it comes out right when your check does so you're not going to be overdrawn, and you can change it at any time. So which day would work best?"** That's how you handle those weak ones, and you get a sense for it after you've done it a lot.

But you'll get the occasional ones which are "I'm not doing a bank draft." At that point you would basically say something similar to what I said as far as rebuttal-ing that objection and see where that leads you. At that point, if you have a carrier, a direct bill, some of them do direct bill. There's very few that do.

The reason I don't offer that without a little bit of fight is because your pay is probably going to be as-earn with most companies on a direct bill basis. So I don't even fool with it. What I do is just go for the bank draft if at all possible. After that's done, once I wrap that up, I get that information. Usually I can get over those objections. If I can't, you offer a money bill option or you tell them they've got to pay quarterly. You just put it out there. Because you've got to work smart as well as work hard, and if they're just not going to play ball, then what are you going to do? You give it a shot; if it's not going to work, at this point they're this resistant, there's not much you can really do.

At this point, once you're done there, to move on, we move into the summary wrap up stage. This is where you summarize everything that you've discussed with the prospect, now who's your client. You review when to expect the literature in the mail, the policy, and then kind of what to expect next so as to keep them abreast of where this is going. My script and my approach is as follows:

I say, "**Mr. Jones, what I'm going to do is leave behind this brochure. I'm going to write out all the information, the most important points, so you have that in hand before your policy** comes. In the meantime, you've been pre-approved for coverage. If there's any issues, I will call you directly and go over it with you. 9 out of 10 times there's not, so you won't hear from me until after you've received your policy – which again, takes about two to three weeks. We'll call you back, and the reason I'll call is just to make sure you got your policy and just to make sure that you're totally happy and completely satisfied."

That's what I tell them there, so they know what to expect.

Then I'll say, "**Mr. Jones, again, just to make sure, just to summarize, I just want to go over the main points of the policy. Again, #1, your coverage is for $10,000. That's Day 1 100% coverage that you've been pre-approved for. It covers you for the first day the policy is enforced. Secondly, your rate is $50 a month. Again, that rate never goes up, period. Ever. It's always the same for the rest of your life. The draft date that you've picked is the 4th, starting next month in October, and that's the date it's always going to be. If the 4th is on a weekend, it'll come out on that Monday, only because the banks are closed, so that way you won't ever get hit before that day. But for every other normal day, it comes out on the 4th. Then lastly, you cannot be canceled because of age or any changes in health. My number is down there at the bottom.**"

Then I'll tell them at that point, "**I circled some things inside the**

brochure so that you know which policy's yours." Little details like that, just to catch their eyes if they're reviewing it, if they're going back and looking through things to make sure everything looks legit.

At this point, I'll say, **"Mrs. Jones, do you have any other questions or any concerns with what you got?"** And I'll let them tell me if there's any issues, if they have double checking about their prices or anything like that, or coverage amount. Then if they say "No, everything looks good," I'll say, "Mrs. Jones, how do you feel about what you did today? How do you feel about taking this policy out?" I'll let them tell me. I want them, in their own words, to tell me that this was a good choice. "Do you feel like this is a good policy?

Do you feel good about this?" I want them to have total buy-in before I leave the house.

The point of doing all this is to ensure that I have somebody who's going to keep their policy. Because when you sell these policies, there is still a chance the applicant can change her mind and not pay the first premium. Things can happen in between you leaving and them getting their policy and the first payment being made. So you want to make sure you take the time to go over those things when you're talking to the customer.

At that point, once you review, a good tactic to do at this point is called the cool down. The point of doing this is to reconnect as a human and not on the basis of business. Keep it simple. Talk about anything unrelated to business.

Follow Up And Administrative Work

Once you close the business, that's not the end of the story. You've got to go through the next several stages to make sure that the closed business stays, because the policy that stays is the policy that pays, as one final expense agent said. Here's how to take care of keeping business after you close it, with following up and with back office work.

The first of which is the follow-up. The follow-up is loosely what I describe as just making sure that the client knows that you're there, that you're not going away, that you're staying on top of things, and that you're keeping and retaining the trust that you had when you left the house. My follow-up schedule as an agent is pretty simple: I follow up right about two to three weeks, maybe even four weeks after the policy is closed with a simple phone call where I just introduce myself, ask them how they're doing that day, just a little chit-chat, and then asked them if they've received the policy and if they have any questions.

My follow-up at that point is on an annual basis, although you can more or less do it semi-annually, even quarterly. I don't think there's a level of follow-up that is overboard, because the agent that's going to do the most follow-up is the one that's going to earn referrals, is the one that's going to keep business, and have better persistency. So there's really nothing to say that you can't do any of that as far as the frequency of follow-ups. Always, when you do an interaction with a client, always ask if they have a name or two, friends or family members that you could call on to discuss life insurance with. It's just a great opportunity, especially if you've done something where you've helped them out, maybe with fixing a beneficiary or some sort of activity like that. Just something to keep in mind.

As far as back office work, this really pertains to making sure that the policies that you submit are received, and then also to make sure the policies that are received are processed in a timely manner. Sometimes the home office can get a backup of policies and not process them correctly, and they won't let you know, and so that's more reason that you have to stay on top of the business that you submit. A couple of things you can do is every morning, check the status of your policies. Most carriers have back office sites where you can see how they're pending and why they're pending and what needs to be completed, if you need a new signature or if you forgot a form. That way you can just stay on top of your business to make sure it's submitted correctly in a timely fashion.

Because the worst thing you could have happen is a policy that's in limbo for several weeks, past the day it was supposed to draft, and then not draft because it's in pending. Then the policy gets drafted several weeks after, the client calls mad because they didn't have money in the bank account, and you look like the bad guy. Long story short, utilize your back office work to make sure your policies are getting taken care of, they're being submitted in a timely fashion, and if anything pops up, like a lapse, a chargeback, mis-payment, you can see those things and act on that, which really is a very crucial component to maintaining your business.

One thing I found with agents I've talked to is this whole section is one of the most neglected. Most agents that sell final expense are kind of in the mold of an outside sales, business to business guy. They go out, they find it, and they kill it, bag it and tag it and go to the next one. Their level of relationship building is not necessarily the best, only because that's the nature of how this business is; we go out and we sell and we go to the next one.

I had to personally discipline myself to do this back office work because it's so important, and because I've lost a lot of money by not staying on top of it over my beginning. What I would recommend is, in order to do this successfully, whenever you see a lapse, whenever you see a cancelation, whenever you see anybody trying to get rid of their policy, purposely or non-purposely, that is a reason to call. That is a reason to follow up, and that is a reason to either fight to retain the business or to ask for referrals.

A lot of the lapses, a lot of the non-payment issues are human error. There might have been a bank draft number incorrectly written recorded. I have seen where that's been an issue on a $2500 commission I've had on account a year ago. I ignored till three months later and realized that the client just had the wrong bank draft number on there, and she never called me – again, because these people don't call you back; that's why you have to stay on top of it. When I went and dropped by her house, she said that she felt like they just didn't want her anymore, which is not the case. It was just a simple error.

With all that said, the bottom line is when you see a lapse, call them up; a lot of times, it's a simple mistake. They can restart it, drop it to the next month. Most carriers are flexible and will work with you to make sure that that actually happens. But don't lose money, because I have in the past where I've lost business to other agents or the clients weren't interested anymore, and some of it I won back. But the most important thing is just you've got to make sure that anything that happens like that, you stay on top of. Because it is fixable. It's not always a losing scenario. But that's the best way to maintain your persistency levels to a satisfactory level.

Summary

At the conclusion of this book, I hope you have garnered a new found respect and understanding of what the final expense business is about and also what this business is about from a mindset perspective and a relational perspective between you and your agency. It's extremely important that you understand and hopefully, you have gained this perspective that you must set up your career in final expense not just for short-term gain, but ultimately for long-term gain because making one wrong move can make all the difference in the success of failure of your business.

And now you know exactly how final expense leads work, what your options are, and who the preferred people are to work with. You also know what to look for in working with agencies so you can avoid getting the short end of the stick. You now know how to prospect and set appointments over the phone and door knock in person and you also have a great understanding, a detailed understanding, of how final expense sales work and what to look for and how to sell successfully to each one of your prospects and clients.

My hope is that you enjoyed this book, and the most important thing for me is to give out content in a book that's actionable, that gets you results, that when you do it, you can see an improvement in your game and in your bottom line bank account. If you have any questions, feel free to visit me at my website at http://www.FEAgentMentor.com if you're interested in joining or possibly working with my organization.

I've got a YouTube page with lots of free videos which you can check out, much of which I talk about in video format there. Go to YouTube and put in 'Final Expense Agent Mentor' and you will see the hundreds of videos I have that help explain this video. Thanks so much for listening, take care.

Recommended Reading

Book #1: *Atlas Shrugged* by Ayn Rand: A foundational philosophical and moral book that I read (or listened to, really) as a young man that made a profound impact on my life. Highly recommended for all of those out there who are looking for guidance on perspective in philosophy and why businessmen like you and I are an indispensable asset for the welfare of society at large.

Book #2: *The E-Myth Revisited* by Michael E. Gerber: A book I read very long ago helped me conceptualize the importance of building a business that is built upon the concepts of a franchise; how to develop a business that isn't dependent upon one person, singularly, but operates independently of you because of the systems that you put in place.

Book #3: Brian Tracy's *Advanced Selling Strategies:* A very important sales book that helped me understand sales from a business to consumer standpoint. I have read the book a multitude of times. Brian Tracy is an excellent lecturer and thinker in the sales business. Anything that he writes is good, but this one in particular made the biggest impact on me in my very beginnings as an agent.

Book #4: Claude Whitacre's *One Call Closing:* Claude Whitacre is a vacuum salesman, but also a consultant for sales and marketing for retail operations. I have never met Claude personally, but his teaching is so unique from most of the sales teaching out there because it's actionable, it's something that really works in a business to consumer environment and is something that I would definitely recommend all people do because of how simple his concepts are and how well he explains how it works so that you can better understand it.

Book #5: *Selling for Dummies* by Tom Hopkins: This is one of the first sales books I got. It's a good primer to understand how sales works traditionally and how to develop an approach to selling.

Anything by Steven Schiffman. Steven Schiffman is a corporate sales trainer, he's been around for a long time. He doesn't have the same level of notoriety as some of the other people I've mentioned, but his material is very good to understand some basics to sales that isn't hokey or corny. Very good at teaching how to set appointments, very good at managing sales cycles-- a little more applicable to the B2B world, but some basic information in there is very useful for someone selling something as straight forward as burial insurance.

Dan Kennedy's No B.S. Book series: All of his books are great to understand marketing, as well as sales. He has a very good understanding of the takeaway approach to selling and to make yourself more useful or more perceived to be standing apart from the competition.

The Ultimate Sales Machine is one of the better strategy books on selling by the late Chet Holmes. He passed away at a very young age, but had a great profound impact on how to sell in such a way.

Ayn Rand's *Capitalism the Unknown Ideal:* Very good information on understanding capitalism and respect for the people like myself and you who want to go out there and make money and why we're good and not bad people.

55070365R00108

Made in the USA
Lexington, KY
09 September 2016